THE UNIQUE WORLD
OF WOMEN

THE
UNIQUE
WORLD OF
WOMEN

...in Bible Times and Now

EUGENIA PRICE

MAIN STREET BOOKS

DOUBLEDAY
New York   London   Toronto   Sydney   Auckland

A MAIN STREET BOOK
PUBLISHED BY DOUBLEDAY
a division of Bantam Doubleday Dell Publishing Group, Inc.
1540 Broadway, New York, New York 10036

MAIN STREET BOOKS, DOUBLEDAY, and the portrayal of a building with a tree are
trademarks of Doubleday, a division of
Bantam Doubleday Dell Publishing Group, Inc.

The Unique World of Women was previously published by
Zondervan Publishing House in 1969. The Main Street edition is published by
arrangement with Eugenia Price.

ISBN 0-385-41715-2

contents

New Testament

PREFACE

This book was written nearly a quarter of a century ago. Does it still make sense for today's woman? Yes, because although the kinds of women found in these pages are outwardly far different from women today, God does look on the heart. Our wills are being freed, and our choices, but hearts remain the same.

Women are much freer now to choose for themselves, but no matter how successful we become or even if the "glass ceiling" finally gives way entirely under our upward pressure, in one way, the world of women will remain unique. Women are not men. Men are not women, but that surely isn't the point of this book. God does not change, and He is surely still speaking to us through the women of the Bible.

In these pages, written so long ago, you will see the start of a budding novelist. I have chosen to write short "stories" and then meditations on the little-known women of the Bible. Thanks to amazingly understanding parents, I have always been free to choose freely for myself—not to marry if I chose, to marry if I chose. Above all, to work at becoming whatever fulfilled *me*. I decided on an absorbing career instead of marriage, but the decision was entirely mine. I was never made to feel peculiar simply because even over sixty years ago I didn't automatically do what most of my high-school classmates did. All my seventy-seven years, I have been a "liberated woman," but with the same heart needs, the same personality quirks, the same fears and anxieties native to all women. To all people.

The saving grace for the entire human race is the vastness of God's love, His infinite sensitivity to each one of us, His singular, incomprehensible inclusive art of encompassing us all. To encompass us, to guide us, to be our best friend and to keep on speaking to us today. The greatest grace may be that He knows above everyone else that we all need to go on listening.

EUGENIA PRICE
St. Simons Island, Georgia
May 1993

THE UNIQUE WORLD
OF WOMEN

Women of the Old Testament

Keturah

... loving enough to be second

Keturah

...loving enough to be second

Keturah lifted the flap of Abraham's black goatskin tent and stood looking at him as he lay on his bed of soft rugs. His eyes were closed, his gray-streaked beard wet with tears. He looked old.

He is old, Keturah thought. My beloved husband is old. As old as he is dear to me. She smiled, remembering her dreams as a girl — dreams that always centered around a strong, tall young man with a thatch of curly black hair — a lithe, straight lover who held her in smooth, hard arms, who laughed proudly when he returned from hunting, bringing her the biggest stag of all.

Keturah was young, perhaps not as beautiful as she hoped she would be, but young, firm-breasted, full of life, married now — not to her tall imagined hunter — to ancient Abraham, who lay on his bed much of the time, rousing only when she came to him, reminding him that he was no longer alone.

"You are crying again, my husband," she said softly, as to a child. "Aren't you ashamed of yourself? Especially now that you are the father of our fourth son, Midian."

He opened his pale, old eyes.

11

"Shall I bring Midian in to you?" she asked cheerfully.

"No, Keturah. You are enough."

"If I am enough, Abraham, why do you cry so often?"

The old man sighed. "I dreamed about *her* just now when I dozed off. She was here again. When I woke up, I wept."

Sarah. Abraham would always love her. Keturah knew that when she married him. Sarah, his first wife, would always be his real wife to him. He had loved his son, Ishmael, by Sarah's tragic maid, Hagar, and he loved the four sons Keturah had given him, but Sarah and her son, Isaac, would always be first.

"I miss my son, Isaac, now that he has married and gone away, Keturah."

"Of course, you do. It wouldn't be natural if you didn't."

"Isaac, my son, is gone and his mother, Sarah, is gone too."

Keturah laid her hand on his forehead, then leaned down to kiss him. "If I could, I would bring them both back to you, my husband."

He looked at her. "Sarah was not as unselfish as you."

Keturah laughed. "I am not really unselfish. I just love you so much your happiness is more important than mine."

"Do I make you unhappy, child?"

She smiled. "Do I look unhappy?"

Abraham sighed again and patted her arm. "Bring our new son, Midian, now, Keturah. I must learn to live in the present. Bring Zimran and Jokshan and Medan, too. I want all my sons around me — all the sons left to me now that Isaac is gone."

Keturah ran to get the children, her heart singing with joy. At least she had given him four sons. Soon she would tell him another child was on its way. Maybe, the Lord God would send him a fifth son. Enough sons might help to make up for Isaac's absence.

12

Her husband was up when she returned with the new baby and the other three boys. He was up off his bed, his face washed, his old eyes dancing with anticipation. As he embraced one after another of the noisy children, the years seemed to drop away. His shoulders were still bent, but he made an effort to stand straight. His hands were blue-veined and thin, but they took on strength as he grasped each stalwart son approvingly by the shoulders.

When she laid the youngest son in Abraham's arms, the old man looked up at her and smiled. This smile was just for her. There were moments when she knew he was giving her his full attention, when he was living in the present with her and their children. The moments didn't come often, but when they came, they were enough. Keturah loved him as a father, as a child to care for, and as a husband. She was blessed, she decided. After all, if she had found the strong, young hunter she had dreamed of as a girl, she might have been able to love him only one way.

She watched Abraham play with his sons and her heart was glad — glad for the new child within her, hopeful for still another. She would never be first with her husband, but he would always be first with her, and for Keturah this was enough.

* * * * * * * * *

As I re-created this little episode about Keturah, I thought of another woman about whom I wrote in my first novel laid on St. Simons Island. A woman who, like Keturah, really lived and made the most of her second place in the heart of the man she loved: Anna Gould Dodge, the second wife of the Rev. Anson Greene Phelps Dodge in *The Beloved Invader*. In fact, Anna's unselfishness, her ability to love totally for love's sake, was the first aspect of this true story which interested me enough to write the novel. Anna, like Keturah, had no delusions about the kind of love her husband felt for her. Both

13

men loved their second wives, but both men would always love their dead wives more. Both men respected their second wives, cared for them, and were true to them, but romance was missing. Both men needed their second wives, and the wives were willing to fill the needs exactly as they were. Neither Anna Dodge nor Keturah demanded to be first. They were realistic, and they loved enough to find joy in their lot.

Many persons — perhaps most persons who have lost their mates in death — marry again out of loneliness, needing someone to talk to, someone with whom to travel, someone to fill the empty chair at the dinner table, the empty bed. This is natural. The habits of companionship and conversation and shared joys and irritations do not vanish when the loved one is gone. The one left behind remains the same, with the same needs and the same longings.

Second marriages aren't always successful, but it is perfectly natural for a man to want another wife or for a woman to want another husband once the sharp edge of the grief has worn down. The trouble begins when either member of the second marriage expects to be worshiped and adored and made to feel all important. He or she is just not going to be exactly like the first partner, and so a whole new adjustment must be made on both sides.

In the story of Keturah, though (as with Anna Dodge), the adjustment had to be made mostly on the woman's side. Both women had to love enough so that their joy was dependent — not upon their own fulfillment, their own happiness — but on the fulfillment and happiness of their husbands. Keturah and Anna faced their positions as second wives realistically and made the most of what they did have. Neither, I believe, did this passively. They did not sigh and resign themselves to their second fiddle roles. They did what they could do creatively, with no sign of self-pity. Anna Dodge went so far as to have her

14

husband's mother buried beside him and his first wife in the plot he had reserved for Anna. Keturah went so far as to accept, apparently, the fact that Abraham settled only gifts on her sons while leaving full hereditary rights to Sarah's one son, Isaac.

I like Keturah. She wasted no energy fighting her second place; she grasped it in both hands and redeemed it.

Deborah, the nurse

...a life of giving love

Genesis 24:59; 35:8

Deborah, the nurse

...a life of giving love

Deborah was old and full of years — years crowded with memories. Not memories of her own children, of her own husband, of her own home; she had never known a husband, had never had children of her own. Still, nearing her ninetieth birthday, as she sat before her own tent drowsing a bit in the hot summer sun, she did not feel that life had robbed her.

Since her youth, Deborah had belonged to a family she loved, and who loved her. Her belonging had gone far beyond the state of slavery into which she had been born, and God had greatly blessed her. To have been chosen to nurse and care for Rebekah, the lovely child of her master, Nahor, was reason enough for a full life for Deborah. She had gone with Rebekah the day she left her father's house to journey to Canaan where she was to marry Abraham's beloved son, Isaac. To Deborah, it was as though she, too, were preparing herself for marriage. She knew at once that Rebekah would love Isaac. They had seen him meditating in his fields as their caravan rolled along the sandy road toward Abraham's lands. She loves him, Deborah thought. My beautiful

19

Rebekah loves this man of fine countenance. Of course, he will love her too. And I will be able to watch their love grow with the years. I will know the joy of nursing their children.

Deborah sat before her tent remembering Rebekah and Isaac that warm, summer day, and she smiled. Then a frown creased her lined old forehead, as the moment of her first disillusionment flashed through her mind. How she had tried to explain away — even to herself — what her mistress Rebekah did the day she forced her favorite son, Jacob, to trick both his blind father, Isaac, and his unsuspecting brother, Esau. Deborah had not been able to explain it away. The woman she had almost worshiped had done an evil thing. If she were honest, there was only one way to look at it — the way it was. Well, Deborah had reasoned within herself, my mistress simply loves her son Jacob so much she can't bear her other son, Esau, to have the birthright. I cannot condemn her. I must go on trying to understand her. Deborah loved Jacob too. He was handsomer than Esau, more delicately made, brilliant, sensitive, and attentive to his mother. Deborah had nursed and cared for Esau, and although she felt him equally as lovable as Jacob, she understood Rebekah's favoritism. Jacob was more like his mother. It was only natural that they were close, and that Rebekah would do anything to see to it that Jacob had the best his father had to offer. Still, Deborah's heart had ached for blind, aging Isaac and for big, redhaired, blundering Esau. And never again did she respect Rebekah as before. She still loved her, but there was an emptiness from that day on in Deborah's heart where the respect had been.

20 Her old head bobbed a little as the warm sun and the overwhelming depth of her memories tired her. She slept a few minutes, then awoke sharply as once more she relived the pain of Rebekah's heartbreak the night her be-

loved son Jacob had to run away like a criminal in the dark. Esau had discovered the deception and had vowed to kill his brother. Rebekah had paid dearly for what she had done. By grabbing for him what was not rightly his, she had lost her favorite son.

Deborah always let her mind leap over the dark moment when news reached her of Rebekah's death. The deaths of Isaac and Rebekah had been painful for her. When she sat sorting her memories, as she did often now that her working days were over, she had never once dwelt on those sorrowful days.

Instead she would think about the day when she came to live with Jacob and his first wife Leah, the woman he didn't want. The watery-eyed, homely elder daughter of Laban, his uncle, who had tricked Jacob as Jacob had tricked his brother Esau. Being with Jacob again was almost like having her mistress, Rebekah, back. He was as lovable as his mother had been — as scheming, she knew — but in Jacob, Deborah saw, as the years went by, great hope. The day he told her about his vision, about the night he wrestled with the Lord God, Deborah knew that God would somehow be able to make a whole man of Jacob. As she watched him work in Laban's fields for the second seven years so that he could marry the lovely Rachel, she saw his capacity for love.

Faithfully, as though they, too, were her own children, Deborah nursed Jacob's children by the plain, hard-working Leah. Then his first child by Rachel was born. Deborah held the baby, Joseph, and thanked God. Her joy was great, especially as she saw Rachel's joy and Jacob's pride, but Deborah had never been able to banish the fear that was always there beside her joy. Rachel was too beautiful, too much in love with Jacob — their happiness seemed too perfect to last. 21

I'm only growing old and anxious, Deborah would tell herself, but the fear did not go away. Rachel would soon give birth to Benjamin, her second son, and old Deborah was afraid. Somehow she must live to help Rachel when her second child came, but death, her own death, seemed suddenly sweet.

* * * * * * * * * *

Death came for ancient Deborah before she could help Rachel, and we are told that Jacob buried the old woman under an oak tree near Bethel. He named the tree *The Oak of Weeping*, and this tells us everything about Deborah as a human being. An aged slave woman, no longer able to work, could easily have been only a burden to the nomadic Jacob. Deborah was not a burden. She had always been a burden-bearer, and when she died, Jacob and his family wept so much that he called the oak above her grave Allon-bachuth — *Oak of Weeping*.

Behind the counters in department stores, in schoolrooms, at typewriters in business offices, at home caring f)r an elderly parent — or bereft and lost when the parent has died at last — one can find single women with brittle, empty hearts. Brittle because they feel life has passed them by. They have had no husband to love them, to provide for them, to give them companionship, and, of course, no children to watch grow or to care for them in their old age. Many of these unmarried women become bitter. Being a single woman myself, by choice, I feel I have not understood their bitterness until I had spent some time with Deborah. And by contrast, I have come to see why a woman might become embittered if she has for one reason or another been deprived of children of her own.

Deborah has helped me understand the women who are bitter without a husband and children simply by the example of her long life. Deborah, born into slavery, spent her years serving others, nursing other women's children. I don't think Deborah was necessarily what we loosely call "a saint." That she was an unselfish, caring

22

person is obvious. But first of all, I think Deborah was a *realist*. She had been born into slavery. She was going to have to spend her entire life in the service of other people. There was absolutely nothing she could do about it, and so she faced the facts of her life. She accepted it as it was and turned all her creativity and her energy into making it — not bitter and burdensome — but beautiful. Deborah could have worked just as hard as she did work, could have given of her time and body to the children who were under her care, could have been available when needed, but at the same time, she could have, if she had chosen, rebelled, grown bitter, and shouted at God in the silence of her servitude that He should have done better by her.

I know one woman near my own age — know her rather well — who has been an excellent employee all her life, has done her work carefully and well, has been generous and helpful to her neighbors, gives almost compulsively (depriving herself often) to the support of missionaries, is rabid in her church attendance, and yet, she is one of the most miserable, quick-tempered, critical people I know. She is, of course, single and alone. She has *done* outgoing things, but the outgoingness has not come from inside. It is as though, if it kills her, she will do these things that cause people to commend her. I would have felt cruel writing this a few years ago. But I have watched her grow more tight-lipped, clutching her rigid life pattern closer by the day, and in the process, she is wearing down those few friends who have tried for years to tread softly around her personality. She is a "good" woman, whatever that means. But she is miserable, incapable of having any fun, as though she is afraid if she really laughed, she might crack.

Deborah could have grown bitter. Undoubtedly, she was born with a special love for children. Never to have borne a child might well have made her more rebellious

23

than most. She was not rebellious. If she had been, she would not have remained important to the members of Jacob's family even after she had grown too old to serve. Deborah evidently stayed lovable. They didn't want her to go away. Even though she was ninety years old, everyone still wanted to have her around!

I drove past the little cemetery near my house not long ago, and when I pointed out a graveside service, a friend riding with me said, "Oh, I hope it's someone very old, so no one will grieve much."

This is too often the way it is, but not with Deborah. Somehow along the way, she had learned how to allow the Lord God to teach her creative acceptance. They all wept when she died. They would miss her — not her service, for that had ended long ago. They missed Deborah herself.

Judith and Bashemath

...Rebekah's troublesome daughters-in-law

Judith and Bashemath

Rebekah's troublesome daughters-in-law

Rebekah's faithful nurse, Deborah, had no daughters-in-law of her own, but she was not unfamiliar with the problems they can bring into a household. She was also not unfamiliar with the problems their mother-in-law can make for them.

"You have been my loyal friend and nurse for all these years, Deborah," Rebekah would wail. "I demand that you take my side in this dreadful business of having those two heathen women in my household! Married to my own son, Esau — my boorish, ungrateful, headstrong son. So unlike his gentle brother, Jacob. Trouble enough I've had from Esau alone. Now, he adds to my sorrow by bringing two Hittite wives to live right under my nose. Deborah! I demand that you sympathize with me."

Deborah did sympathize with her mistress, but she also sympathized with Esau and his two wives. In her heart, she was on Rebekah's side, but in her quiet, balanced mind, she must have seen the problem whole.

Not much is known about Judith and Bashemath, but they were probably beautiful. Esau was not a fool and he was certainly a desirable husband: a skillful hunter, a

27

magnificent physical specimen, pleasure-loving, and the son of Isaac, one of the wealthiest and most respected patriarchs. Both Judith and Bashemath had to leave their own homes, their own land, to go with their husband, Esau, but both of them evidently thought him worth it.

Judith and Bashemath were not sisters, although both came from Canaan, of pagan Hittite families. Judith, the daughter of Beeri, and Bashemath, the daughter of Elon. Both men, although idolatrous, with no knowledge of the Lord God, were evidently well-off. There is no reason to believe that on his pleasure jaunts into the godless land of Canaan Esau would have been attracted to women not as well born as he. Esau also went into his marriages with his eyes open. He knew his parents would both be more than upset at his choices. They were more than upset. His marriages were a "grief of mind unto Isaac and Rebekah." So far as anyone knows, neither parent ever got over it.

"We are believers in the Lord God, Isaac," Rebekah would repeat over and over to her husband. "How could our son do this to us? Wasn't he reared in the faith as his brother Jacob? Look at Jacob! He has married within his own people — just what one could expect of a fine son like Jacob. But look at Esau! Day in and day out we have to contend with the presence of these two sinful creatures right in our own household, Isaac!"

Isaac would sigh heavily and bow his head. "I know, Rebekah. I know, I know, I know. Do you not think I know what Esau has done? Do you not think I live here, too, day in and day out with these shameless women worshiping their idols, performing their evil dances and rituals? But what is there to do, Rebekah? What is there to say?"

28

"I'll tell you what there is to say," Rebekah would snap back. "This is just what one would expect of that wild-horse son of yours!"

And often Rebekah would weep. One day, years after Jacob had gone and Esau had married the Hittite women, Deborah found Rebekah prone on her bed, her shoulders shaking with the sobs she could not control.

"Is it what Esau has done, Mistress?" Deborah whispered, smoothing Rebekah's hair. "Is it only what Esau has done by marrying these two Hittite women that troubles you? Or is it because your favorite son, Jacob, is gone from my master's household?"

Sitting up suddenly in the middle of her bed, old Rebekah stared at her nurse. "That will be enough of that, Deborah! You do not make me comfortable by reading my mind. I insist that you stop it." And then the old woman fell back on her pallet. "It is both," she sighed. "It is because I have lost Jacob that I weep. But it is because I have these two evil women with me that I grow angry enough to show it. I will live out the remaining years of my life bearing the absence of Jacob, my beautiful son, and the grief and sorrow of the presence of my evil son, Esau, and his two heathen wives!"

Deborah said nothing as she spread a light coverlet over her mistress and sponged the tears from her wrinkled old face.

"It is doubly grievous, Deborah," Rebekah whispered, "because I am old. I am too old to look forward to peace again. My life will be over soon and before me there is only grief."

* * * * * * * * * *

Most of the commentators I have read on Rebekah and her two daughters-in-law are sympathetically pro-Rebekah and anti-Esau, anti-Judith and Bashemath.

What I have to say is neither for nor against any one of them. I believe we only begin to understand the purpose of some of these Old Testament stories when we do three things. First, we must remember they were written in a period very different from ours — written and lived out in an ancient time unfamiliar to us. Second, stop trying to be so literal in our application of these stories when we attempt to discover what God might be saying to us today. And third, keep in mind that these people had far more reason to be unpleasant, impatient, evil, clannish, self-righteous, and idolatrous because Jesus Christ had not yet come to reveal the Father's true nature or to make possible the gift of the permanent indwelling Holy Spirit. These people, Abraham and Sarah, Rebekah and Isaac, were believers in the Lord God, but as far as having access to the balance or love or wisdom of the indwelling Spirit of God as we have now, they were living out their daily lives pretty much on their own. They lived in such closely knit tribes, that to keep the purity of the line, the form of family worship, family custom and tradition intact and untouched from outside was their one goal. In our period, we can still find remnants of this old tribal habit of mind. I find it in the South (United States) where I now live. It exists in New England and among ethnic groups in the Middle and Far West. "We want to keep everything just the way it's always been. Those of us who are Swedish or German or southern or white or Protestant or Catholic should stay together. We can be courteous to outsiders, but let's not go too far." It has surprised me, and many of my Yankee friends don't believe it, but I have found this among certain of my black neighbors in Georgia who are older descendants of ante-bellum slaves. They are not what we know from the press and TV as anti-white "black militants," either. They are just set in their own patterns, their own church habits, their own kind of music; they keep intact an island aristocracy among a select group of blacks which closes out even 30 other blacks who didn't happen to have been born on St. Simons Island. There are three cemeteries for Negroes here. In two of them, the Gould cemetery and the King's Retreat burial ground, *only* those related at least by marriage to a slave descendant are permitted to lie down at last. In the third graveyard, the Stranger's Cemetery, "outsiders" may be buried. This seems to cause no problems. It is merely an accepted tribal custom. And "outsiders" are those who may have been born near Darien, Georgia, just fifteen miles up the mainland. One day all this will be forgotten, but remnants do remain. I recall several years ago when I was speaking in an Evangelical Covenant church on the west coast, the minister said proudly: "Look at our congregation this morning. We have five black faces, two East Indians, and a Japanese! We're not going to stay exclusively Swedish in this church forever."

They won't.

In the days of the nomadic patriarchs, it was a real switch when two women from one tribe — the Hittites — married a man from another. When Judith and Bashemath left their fathers' households in Canaan to spend the rest of their lives with Esau in the household of Isaac — "right under Rebekah's nose" — it was a distinct departure from custom.

Esau did a foolish and a selfish thing when he married outside the faith of his fathers. Not only did he cause great grief and bitterness and sorrow for his aging parents, but he caused endless trouble for his wives too. Rebekah, although we agree with her theologically and disagree with the idol worship of Judith and Bashemath, must have been just as difficult for them as they were for her.

As always, in order to draw realistic, practical conclusions, we must look at both sides. I feel strongly that in order to get a true perspective on any trouble, any problem — surely in order to discover something of what God might be saying to us as women today — we must make an effort to be objective.

31

Taking into full account the fact that old Rebekah was truly heartbroken — the grief of Esau's selfishness added to the grief she already carried because her favorite Jacob had to run away — we must find some point of identification with her daughters-in-law too. We agree with Rebekah's doctrine, but I feel we must also agree with the two younger women's plight. They were in a rough spot. True, they didn't have to come. Surely they knew Esau came from a household of faith in the Lord God. There is always the chance, of course, that he neglected to tell them, since Esau's faith wasn't exactly a shining flame. Whatever the circumstances — whoever was to blame — they married the man, and they came to live with his parents. Daughters-in-law in those days had one big advantage over many now, by the way. Mothers seemed always to *want* their sons to marry. So, Rebekah would have had no objections to Esau's bringing home his wives — *if* they had not been Hittites. But they were Hittites, and Rebekah excluded them from her heart and as much as possible from her household.

Now with these points as background, let's get to what I believe God is saying to us today. I do not think the main point of the story is that Esau sinned or that Rebekah and Isaac were "put upon." Neither do I think Esau's selfishness is the point. I agree that the incident can be taken as a reminder that it is neither wise nor kind to try to mix oil and water — either ancestrally or theologically. I do not disagree necessarily with some who insist that the main message is the sin of mixed marriage. It seems to me that this is not the principal issue. At least, I find one that does far more for my own faith in Jesus Christ than a merely laid down law or bit of wisdom: I think the incident is recorded so that we will have still another reason to rejoice!

Think it through with me. It takes no great imagination to see how frustrated, how grieved, how deeply troubled Rebekah was under these impossible circumstances. Neither does it require any extra imagination to reconstruct the daily irritation, the homesickness, the strangeness of heart in both Esau's wives. This was a horrible situation for all concerned. The kind one wants to run from. I'm sure both Judith and Bashemath often wanted to run as hard as they could out across the desert — anything to get away from Rebekah's criticism and woebegone glances — much as Hagar ran from Sarah. But in those days running away was not as easy as it is now. And all Rebekah did, so far as we are told in the Bible, was to complain: "These Hittite women tire me to death!" (Genesis 27:46, Moffatt). She *was* full of sorrow, but she took it out on Isaac, Deborah, Esau, his two wives — and herself.

And this is where our potential for rejoicing comes into the picture. Rebekah did all she *knew* to do. Has it ever made you wonder why the old lady apparently made no effort to win over her son's pagan wives? Even the problem-solving columns in newspapers and women's magazines suggest that someone involved in a bad family relationship try love. We are told nothing of any efforts of this kind either on the part of Rebekah or Isaac. They just lived out their lives in bitterness, and the reason is simple: These people were doing their best to be upright, righteous, faith-filled people, but they *were* doing it on their own. Jesus Christ had not come yet.

I get this from the sketchy story of Rebekah and her two troublesome daughters-in-law: *We* must rejoice. The Son of God has come now. The Spirit of God is loosed in the world now and longs to indwell us — even the disgruntled mothers-in-law among us. Even the homesick, pagan daughters-in-law among us.

No one who is thinking at all could possibly condemn Rebekah, Isaac, Esau, Judith or Bashemath. It was simply a sticky, very human, family mess, and in it they were all powerless from within. We are not. *We are not.*　33

Dinah

. . . a restless teen-ager

Dinah

...a restless teen-ager

In most of the tents of Jacob's household pitched on
the land he had just bought near the Canaanite city of
Shechem, the girl's weeping could be heard. Dinah, her
world smashed around her, lay on her bed, her tousled
head buried in her pillows, her despair and hopelessness
complete. She was the only girl in the family — there
were no sisters near her age with whom she could talk —
and, because she knew her mother was too old and too
plain to understand, she had answered none of Leah's
pleading questions, had refused even to raise her head.
Her life was finished, chopped off at fifteen. Her pain
was final. Her anguish complete. As with all the very
young in trouble, Dinah was drowning in her grief and
remorse.

Quietly, her mother, Leah, slipped out of Dinah's tent
and hurried to their ancient, ailing nurse, Deborah. "Go
in to her, Deborah. Go to my daughter at once! She will
talk to no one — not even to me, her mother — but I believe she will talk to you. I am just old enough to be
too old. You are so far along in years, it may be different.
She may feel you are so heavy with years she can confide

37

in you. I fear for her, Deborah. I know you are ailing, but go to her. If this is the last thing you are able to do for us before you die, please, I beg you, go to my daughter's tent and talk to her."

For a long time Dinah refused to raise her head — still sobbing into her pillows. Old Deborah sat beside her on the bed, waiting. She had patted the girl's head when she first came in, and then she sat down without a word. Her own head ached; her wrinkled, soft skin burned with the fever of her own illness. Deborah was almost ninety and ready to die, but not until she had helped her family through one more crisis. The minutes limped past; the old woman grew dizzy and faint, but she would wait. Over and over she had tried to warn Dinah about the dangers a young girl might face if she left the protection of her own home. Dinah had always been lonely, restless, and shut off from them all inside her own thoughts. It's because she is the only girl among so many brothers, Deborah told herself, but always she had feared it was more than that. Dinah was a rebel. A beautiful rebel, who had matured physically beyond her years. Deborah had tried to rear her properly, and now she had failed. It was hard for an old woman ready to die to experience failure. I must stop dwelling on myself, the old nurse thought. I must wait here with her and pray for her. She waited, dozing a little with her years.

Suddenly Dinah sat up and screamed, "Why?"

Deborah, startled, reached for the girl's hand, but Dinah jerked it away and shouted: "Why! Tell me why this had to happen to me!"

"Sh!"

"Don't sh-h me, old woman! If you're all determined not to leave me alone when I need to be alone, then make yourself useful. Tell me *why* this happened to me!"

"Because you went to Shechem alone, Dinah — that strange, wicked city." Deborah's thin, scratchy voice was

38

as steady as she could make it. "You would still be safe — none of this tragedy would have happened — if you had not wandered off to explore what you were too young to know."

"I don't want a scolding; I want an answer! I found the man I loved, and now he's dead — murdered by my own brothers. I demand to know *why!*"

"There were young men here in your father's household."

Dinah tossed her dark head. "Them! Who was here for me? I'm beautiful, old woman — like my Aunt Rachel — not plain like my mother. When a young woman is beautiful, she deserves more than just some stupid man she's looked at all her life!"

"The Lord God would have supplied."

"Well, He didn't! And now there will never be anyone else for me as long as I live. Prince Shechem was the one man on earth I could have loved. And he loved me, Deborah!"

"He defiled you."

"No!" The girl looked away. "Well, at first. . . . But he did it because he couldn't help himself. He told me, and I knew he was telling me the truth. He just loved me so much the first time he saw me standing in the street of his city looking at some fine silks on sale in the market. He loved me on sight and he — he took me because he was helpless not to. That's love, old woman." Her voice softened. "Always, he spoke tenderly to me. Gently, holding me close. He respected me. He wanted me for his wife — in honor. My own father and brothers made an agreement with Prince Shechem and his father. I was going to live my life as his wife, until Simeon and Levi — did what they did." She shuddered and began to weep again. "Nurse Deborah!"

"What is it, child?"

"I want to die too!"

39

"Hush, Dinah. You're too young to die."

"So was Prince Shechem too young to die. Look what I've done! I've caused the death of my beloved. My own brothers have become murderers. They had never been violent men before this. I did it!" She clung to the old woman. "They weren't satisfied to avenge what they called my honor by killing only the Prince and his father; they murdered every man in Shechem! Murdered every man in the whole city, then stole their herds and stripped their houses, and took all their women and children for their own, so that my poor father will be hated in all the land for having such sons as my brothers! I want to die, old woman. Why can't I die too?"

* * * * * * * * * *

All manner of interpretation has been made of this tragic, violent, confusing story from Genesis. Some writers contend that Jacob, Dinah's father, was being punished for his own chicanery in the past. Others bear down only on Dinah's headlong impulsiveness. They expound at great length on how, in spite of her fine, moral, religious upbringing, she plunged willy-nilly into the wicked city. She did. I have no quarrel with this, but I doubt that it is the way to impress today's teen-agers with the truth that they, too, would be better off to mind their parents.

Actually, I doubt that the story is in the Bible for the purpose of pointing a moral. At least, this is not what strikes me. That the story of Dinah and her pagan Prince Shechem, and all the fearful tragedy that came as a consequence of their loving each other, is one of the most dramatic, human, and realistic episodes in the entire Bible, no one can doubt. I am surprised more has not been done with it dramatically. It is the way so much of life is, if we are honest. Both Dinah and her prince started off on the wrong foot. Both sinned. And yet, it seems equally clear that they loved each other — that Prince Shechem meant to be a good husband to her; meant to care for her

40

and honor her in his household. We are told that ". . . he seized her and lay with her and humbled her." I understand that the Hebrew translation implies he took her by force. And yet, as things turned out, what Prince Shechem did was not actual rape. Seduction, yes, but not rape. If God intended that this turbulent story be used as a guide for the proper behavior for young people, the whole thing could be terribly confusing for them. Thinking of it as a guide, it implies that even though there is premarital relationship, love *can* result. I suppose this is true in some instances, but not generally. So, I think there is a great deal more than a mere moral here.

Much can be written and imagined and deduced about the girl Dinah, the restless teen-ager, who grew bored with the simple, nomadic life of her father's household; Dinah, who wanted so desperately to see a real city, with its lavish shops, beautifully dressed women, and its wide assortment of young men, that she ran away to experience it all for herself. Much has been written along this line, but I'd like for us to consider Jacob, her father — not from the angle of this heartbreak as being his punishment from God for his own past sins. It may be, but I do not see God punishing in this way. And particularly in this story I do not see it. It is the *human* way to punish a man for his sins by inflicting some kind of pain or restriction. As yet, after twenty years as a follower of Jesus Christ, I do not see any instance when God stoops to the level of man's idea of punishment. God punishes by acts of love, and He is doing just that in this story. Flying human emotions and the desire for vengeance brought on the tragedy. Dinah started it, certainly. She was young; her emotions were immature, uncontrolled. She simply did what she wanted most to do. But isn't this true also of her brothers? 41 They were furious that this strange man had defiled their sister, and their uncontrolled fury and vengefulness drove them to murder not only Prince Shechem and a few men close to him, but every man in the city. God didn't prompt them to act this way. Their actions were merely the inevitable consequences of their own hate-filled hearts. Once their fury was unleashed, it mounted until ultimate tragedy fell upon a whole city. Of course, sin operates this way. One misdeed leads to another. This is nothing new.

Jacob, it is true, was heartbroken. He valued his good name, his integrity among his neighbors. He and his household had just moved into a new neighborhood (perhaps another reason Shechem tempted Dinah), and Jacob wanted to be liked and respected. After his sons had run wild in their murderous onslaught against Prince Shechem and his people, Jacob cried out to Levi and Simeon: "You have brought trouble on me by making me odious to the inhabitants of the land, the Canaanites and the Perizzites." The King James Version says: " . . . Ye have troubled me to make me to stink among the inhabitants of the land. . . . " There is no doubt about the extent of Jacob's suffering. Not only his daughter, but all of his sons had shamed him.

Jacob suffered, but God reached down to him to give a fresh start. Long ago, when Jacob was running away from his brother Esau, he made a promise to God which he had never kept. In fact, it would seem that Jacob had slipped a little in his own faith in recent years. At least, we know there were idols in his household (Genesis 35:2). God did not turn away when Jacob needed Him most. He did what I believe He always does in our time of greatest need: He reminded Jacob of the forgotten vow and told him to go to Bethel and build the promised altar to the Lord God. This, the Lord knew, would once more draw the wandering heart of His son Jacob, back to Him. That it got Jacob away from the scene of the tragedy is also very like the Father.

Jesus Christ had not come yet. Calvary had not oc-

42

curred. But God has always been a redeemer God. And sometimes I think, the greater the tragedy, the deeper the trouble, the more opportunity He has to redeem it.

Jacob obeyed. He went to Bethel, fulfilled his promise, and renewed his own closeness to the Lord God.

There was an added benefit to Jacob's having obeyed God in the midst of his own heartache. Old Deborah died, and he was able to bury her lovingly beneath an oak tree near the altar at Bethel.

As with many of the problems teen-agers face today, I believe it is quite possible that Dinah's conduct had been influenced by the indifference of her father, Jacob, to his God.

Tamar

...the widow with her wits about her

Tamar

...the widow with her wits about her

Tamar, tall, slender, her back erect, stood below the high, square window in the thick wall of her father's house and looked up at the sky. Her eyes were quiet; she smiled just a little as she fingered the heavy, gold signet ring, then twirled it round and round on its silken cord. In the corner of her room stood the sturdy, well-worn staff shaped smoothly for a wealthy man from a peeled length of tough, thick vine. Her smile broadened — not unkindly — she was simply maneuvering her rights under the law. The thick staff wouldn't be used until Judah, the well-to-do man who owned it, learned the truth. When he did find out (and one could always trust the village gossips), the staff would be used again, not for walking or climbing, but as the proof she would need. The staff stood in the corner, and she held the signet ring in her hand. There was nothing else to do but wait until it was evident that she was with child, and then she would need both pieces of evidence.

47

Her smile faded a little, and, as though to relate to her own dark memories, a small, dark cloud passed over the sun. Tamar was in her thirties, no longer young, and in her slender body, for the very first time, she carried a child — the child she had longed for, had fought for, but had never managed until now. What she had done to get this child did not disturb her. She was within the custom of the land and later levirate law.

Tamar had been widowed twice. A Canaanite, she had married first Er, the eldest son of Jacob's son Judah, and when he died, she married Onan, Er's brother, as was the custom. On both counts, Tamar lost. Neither man, apparently, was worthy of her. She sighed, still watching the sky change. She had felt lost when each man died, but mainly because they left her childless.

According to the custom of the day, if one husband died, the widow was entitled to marry or to have children by his brother. Judah, her father-in-law, fearing that she was a jinx, she supposed, since both of his sons who had married her were now dead, had put her off in her rightful demand to marry Shelah, his youngest son. "Go back to your father's house and give the boy a chance to grow up," Judah had said, implying that then she would once more have a chance to bear a child — this time by Shelah.

Tamar had gone home to wait, where she waited now, skimming through her dark memories, watching the darkening sky. She was waiting, but not for word from Judah that she could now marry Shelah. This would never come, and Tamar knew it — knew it so certainly that she had put her quick wits into play, and within a few months, she would bear a child — in honor, in complete morality, according to the custom. She smiled again. No one, not even the child's father, knew. Only Tamar, but the time would come. She put the signet ring away in a box, glanced toward the staff leaning in the corner of her room, looked once more at the fading light outside, and lay down on her bed to dream of the child she would hold at last in her arms.

I can wait, she thought, for as long as necessary. Judah

will find out about my unborn child and will send for me to have me burned as a harlot. She went to sleep smiling, unworried, because the signet ring was in its box safe in her room, the staff stood in the corner, and both belonged to the father of her child. The proof of her morality could be denied by no man. She was within her rights, and at last she had found an approved means of becoming a mother.

Sooner than Tamar had hoped, Judah sent for her to be burned as a harlot. A great crowd of people had gathered in the courtyard around Judah's big house, and Tamar was led roughly into their midst, carrying the heavy staff in one hand, clutching the signet ring on its cord in the other.

Erect, her shoulders straight, her proud head high, Tamar stood before Judah, her eyes looking straight into his.

"By the man to whom these belong," she declared, so that everyone could hear, "I am with child." And then she held out the staff and the signet ring. "Mark, I pray you," Tamar went on firmly, "whose these are, the signet and the cord and the staff."

Judah frowned, reached for his staff and his signet ring, looked back at Tamar for a long moment, then lowered his eyes and said, "She is more righteous than I, inasmuch as I did not give her to my son Shelah."

Several months ago Tamar had tricked her father-in-law by masquerading as a harlot beside a road she knew he would be traveling on a sheepshearing trip. Her widow's garments had been folded and put in her chest, and that day she had worn a tantalizing, brightly colored harlot's 49 gown. The device worked. Judah, lonely for a woman since his wife had just died, took her, believing her to be a prostitute. She agreed, of course, but not before he had given her his staff and his signet as a guarantee that he would later give her a kid from his flock.

Now Tamar had humbled Judah; he made no more advances to her, and went so far as to clear her good name before the people. She was within her legal rights, and she used her wits to get those rights. Tamar bore not just one child, but twins, Perez and Zerah. Through Perez, by what to Judah was an illicit moment of self-gratification, Judah and Tamar became ancestors of Jesus Christ. (Matthew 1:3)

✻ ✻ ✻ ✻ ✻ ✻ ✻ ✻ ✻ ✻

I don't think Tamar needs any explaining away. I see no reason why you and I are to be shocked by her little scheme. True, she tricked old Judah, but he certainly asked for it, and don't forget, they lived in the "eye for an eye" era. He must have wanted her very much, or he wouldn't have left his signet ring, the badge of his dignity, with her as security for his payment later. There is no indication that she dragged him into her tent by the side of the road that day. He went willingly. In fact, it was his idea.

To treat the "incestuous" portion is also useless. In this story, as I see it, as with the story of Dinah (as with most of the Old Testament stories), there seems to be no merit in trying to draw mere morals for living today. Our customs are so different from theirs. These were primitive people — more primitive than any writer would dare make them and still keep his Christian reading public! The custom of the day gave Tamar the right to have a son, to keep on trying to have children by first one and then another of Judah's not too distinguished boys. Judah held out on her; he did not fulfill his promise to give her to Shelah, his youngest. The law did not change just because Judah welshed on his bargain. Nor did Tamar's rights change. She simply used her wits, and whether she, or even Judah, was right or wrong morally is not the point at all.

We err when we try to find "lessons" in all these Old
Testament accounts. They are not little "morality plays."
They are records, historical records, however sketchy at
times, of the lives of some of the people of Israel and
their friends and enemies. We are not to try to be like
them or not to be like them. *We are to look for what God
did in all they did.* We are to look for what God did
directly, at the time of their behavior or misbehavior, and
in this story we are to look also for what He dared to do
later. In one sense, He didn't wait to do it. His plan of
redemption was already underway. All through the twilight era of the Old Testament, God was planning, moving
toward the day when He would send His son, Jesus, to
redeem His people from their sins. To give them a way
to live fully, abundantly, without tricks and devices such
as Tamar used.

This is the exciting, overwhelming, humbling message
of the somewhat risqué story of the beautiful Tamar: God
sent His Son through her!

One author said it shocked his "inner, finer feelings to
see Christ's lineage interwoven with such abhorrent deg-
radation. . . . " It definitely does *not* shock mine. It re-
lieves me all the way to the depths of my soul to see that
the Holy God of Israel loved enough to *make use* of ordinary people. I want to shout "hurrah" that He brought
His Son forth through the line of tricky Tamar and lusty
old Judah. This is great good news! This shouts that
God loves with a voice anyone can hear. This declares
once and for all that anyone can be used by God. This
knocks barriers down right and left for those who feel
they are somehow "not good enough to become Christians." This is the Most High God striding across the
earth shouting, "I love! I love! You cannot achieve holi-   51
ness. Nothing you can do by way of morality can bring
us together. By *grace* are you saved."

These same writers who are "shocked" also try to

cushion their shock by insisting upon Tamar's nobility. She was within the law. I quite agree. But she was a conniving woman, a very human woman who was going to get what was coming to her one way or another. She did, and my humanity applauds her. But just as I fail to see how the story can shock, so I fail to see why we have to think of the lovely Tamar as noble. She was just a woman, and she acted like one.

The great, glorious message in this incident has, for me, to do with God Himself. With the infinite caring of God for all of us — good and bad, honest and tricky. God is not shockable. He knows us exactly as we are, and in this knowing, He has done everything possible to open the door to eternal life and love so wide anyone can enter. It did not demean Jesus that Tamar and Judah were His ancestors. *He cannot be demeaned.* But it does help me to get a firmer hold on the irrevocable, freeing truth that God stooped low enough, in Jesus Christ, to reach everyone.

Shiphrah and Puah

...two daring middle-aged women

Shiphrah and Puah

...two daring middle-aged women

After Joseph's death, the descendants of Jacob — Israelites who had come into Egypt — were no longer liked. In fact, they were feared both by the Egyptian people and by their new Pharaoh. "These foreigners are crowding us out of our best land," the Egyptians complained, and wondered what would happen if, in case of war, the Israelites should fight on the side of their enemies. Because the Israelites were a proud people, the Pharaoh decided he could crush their spirits by enslaving them. If that failed, he would find a way to kill them off gradually.

Enslaved, forced to perform backbreaking, menial tasks, the Israelites did not change. They strained their bodies quarrying and moving the great stones with which the pyramids were built, but their spirits seemed only to stretch under the strain. The cruelty of the Pharaoh failed to crush them; rather, it strengthened the strange, seemingly unique bond that held Jacob's descendants apart, aloof even in their enslavement. Something more would have to be done. Their work load was increased. New temples, palaces, treasure-houses, and tombs were built; river embankments were raised; canals and new roads

55

were dug. The Egyptian taskmasters were ordered to whip more often and to require longer hours, but the Pharaoh's hatred and fear of the "foreigners" only grew, as he watched them grow stronger and continue to bear more children.

He would have to take still another step. All the male babies, he decreed, would have to be killed at birth. This would stop the growth of the Israelite population eventually — stop it at its source.

"Bring to me the two chief midwives," the Pharaoh commanded. "Do not bring .any two midwives. I want the two who are in charge of training all such women, in charge of the entire staff of five hundred Egyptian midwives. Bring them before me at once."

Hurrying toward the Pharaoh's palace, the two women talked rapidly to each other, wondering what he could want of them. They were appointed to their profession by the Pharaoh's government, but he had never asked for a face to face consultation with them before.

"Do you think he has discovered that we, his Egyptian subjects, have come to believe in the Israelite God, Puah?" Shiphrah asked, as they bustled up the wide, stone steps of the Pharaoh's court. "Will you admit it, if he has found out?"

Puah glanced at her tall, big-boned fellow worker. "I don't intend to cross that bridge until I'm upon it," she snapped, puffing a little because they were hurrying. "And why are we hurrying so, Shiphrah? My legs are too short to keep up with you."

"I'm hurrying because I want to get it over," Shiphrah whispered sharply, as they rounded the massive stair and started up the long, echoing marble corridor toward the Pharaoh's throne room. "I feel uneasy, and I want to get it behind me."

"But we don't know what he wants," Puah protested.

"I hate suspense, so I'm hurrying. My heart tells me

56

it's bad, whatever it is." Shiphrah walked faster. "Come on, Puah. Stop talking and you can walk faster."

Before the Pharaoh at last, the two women bowed to the ground and then stood erect, waiting for him to speak. He was smiling, toying with his thick, gold bracelets, in no hurry. On his smooth, young face was a look Shiphrah didn't like. Her intuition, she was sure now, had been right.

"Be at ease, women," he said at last. "What I have to say to you is perhaps the most important order you've ever received. As I would give an order to any officer in my government, I now order you to follow to the letter what I command."

Shiphrah and Puah glanced at each other and then back at the Pharaoh. Puah's feet hurt from the long, hurried walk, and she shifted her weight from one foot to the other. Shiphrah stood motionless.

"From this day forward," the Pharaoh said, "every male Israelite child is to be killed at birth."

Puah caught her breath so loudly the Pharaoh heard her and shouted: "Your opinion of my command is of no importance, woman! When you, or any of those who labor under your supervision, serve as midwife to the Hebrew women and see them upon the birthstool, if it is a son, you shall kill him. If it is a daughter, she shall live. That is all. You may go now and begin to carry out my command."

Shiphrah and Puah did not hurry away as they had hurried toward the Pharaoh's palace a few minutes before. Their footsteps lagged as they headed back toward their offices at the school where they trained and supervised the five hundred nurses under them.

All Puah could say was "Shiphrah! Shiphrah, did you hear what he commanded us to do?" 57

"You've said that five times already, Puah. Of course, I heard him. He has asked us to become murderers."

Shiphrah stopped, looking straight ahead, her shoulders very straight. "He has asked us to commit murder, not only against helpless babies who cannot defend themselves, but against the people who taught us to believe in the Lord God of Israel." The taller woman took her friend by the shoulders and turned her so that she could look right in Puah's eyes. "Are you going to obey him?"

Puah's soft, round chin was trembling and her eyes were full of tears.

"Are you going to obey him, Puah?" Shiphrah repeated. "I'm not. Are you?"

That was all Puah needed. "Oh, no, I'm certainly not going to obey such an order. No indeed. No indeed!"

"Good, Puah. Good for you. Your faith in the one true God has held — even in the angry face of that Pharaoh. Come, my friend, I have a plan."

Shiphrah's plan was simply not to kill the boy babies born to the Hebrew women. Most of their work was among the Egyptian women who always had a harder time giving birth than the Hebrew women, but when they attended a Hebrew woman, they simply went about their business as usual. And the boy babies lived and thrived.

When the Pharaoh learned that no Hebrew male children were dying, he called the two plucky midwives before him again. "Why have you done this?" he roared. "Why have you let the male children live?"

Shiphrah and Puah exchanged glances, and Shiphrah replied with feigned seriousness, as though she were imparting a little known medical truth to the Pharaoh: "Because the Hebrew women are not like the Egyptian women, Sire. They are vigorous, and are already delivered before the midwife comes to them!"

58

* * * * * * * * * *

Evidently there was some truth in what Shiphrah said, but in part, at least, she lied. And yet we are told in verse twenty of the first chapter of Exodus that ". . . God dealt with the midwives; and the people multiplied and grew very strong."

Did God "approve" of a lie because the circumstances were so extreme? Do you think there is any point in drawing the conclusion that because God knew Moses was going to be born, because God knew He would select Moses to lead his people out of the bondage of Egypt, away from the cruel Pharaoh, that He condoned Shiphrah's lie? Even being lenient enough toward her to call it a "half-truth," what do you believe God thought about this?

I don't pretend to know in detail. I only know the story of Shiphrah and Puah and their "way out" of their dilemma has made me think.

First of all, I doubt that the real point of the story is to indicate one way or another whether God can go on "dealing well" with us, as the Bible says He did with these two women, if we lie — or if we do not lie. It has seemed for some time to me that everyone would be so much more apt to live *creatively*, if we stopped trying to "get God" to work according to formula — if we stopped trying to live our Christian lives according to formula. In Jesus Christ, God has given no "formula" for creative living. Creative living, to me, is learning to live the gift of our eternal lives right here on this earth. Jesus made a point of admonishing the people about searching the Scriptures (for a formula) and refusing to come to Him personally. Always, He urged the inner life of the Spirit, not the outward life of rules and regulations. My mail is riddled with troubled questions from women, in particular, who are fearful and anxious about whether God *can* forgive this or that breach of regulation. God can forgive anything! This is not the issue. The issue relevant to this little story is that we complicate the life in the Spirit by fretting over the nature of the laws. The nature of the laws is not what matters; it is the nature of God Himself we must study.

I know a man who dissipated his physical energies by living every day to excess — he drank too much, he smoked too much, he ate too much, he kept irregular hours — and yet when he had surgery recently, he got along so well he was up and feeling fine in no time. A woman who had lived a clean, Christian life had basically the same surgery and died. Does this sound as though God was acting according to formula? You know the old saw — and to me it is just an old saw — that God sees to it that we have good health, prosperity, faithful friends, etc. — *as a reward for being good.* Nonsense. Life just does not back this up. And so, one thing which I see emphasized in this incident about the two midwives is that we cannot corner God and predict how He will act in a certain situation. Shiphrah and Puah stretched a point — told at least a "white lie" — but the Bible says "God dealt well with them." This does not give us license to get by on our wits by telling lies. It does indicate that we should act as though we follow a living God, not an ancient parchment covered with little and big laws.

The other thing I see here is that we dare never forget that in this life there will always be choices to make. God knows this. It seems to me that these women had the choice of breaking one or the other of what later came to be known as the Ten Commandments. Of course, too, perhaps we are wasting our time to try to track the morality of these women at all, since even the Ten Commandments had not been given when they lived. Still, life does present predicaments which are neither black nor white — but gray. They had to choose whether to murder or to lie. God knows our limitations — the limitations of our hearts and our spiritual understanding. They chose to lie rather than to kill.

Zipporah

...Moses' inadequate wife

Exodus 2:21 (2:15 - 22; 18:2 - 7)

Zipporah

...Moses' inadequate wife

Zipporah, the daughter of Jethro, a kindly, wise Midianite priest, sat moodily on the ground beside the well, while her six sisters drew water.

"What gives you the right to rest while we pull and haul this heavy water up out of the well, Zipporah?"

"Just because you're going to have a baby is no excuse for laziness!"

"None of the rest of us sit down in the middle of a hard task like this. Get up and do your part!"

Zipporah's sisters were annoyed with her, and they showed it. "You're all just jealous," she answered casually. "It isn't my fault that Moses chose me. I can't help it that he thought me prettier, more desirable."

"We're not jealous! We want you to help us. We're tired too."

"What kind of courtesy would we show to Moses — a cultured Egyptian from a foreign land — if overwork caused his wife to fail at bearing him a child?" Zipporah asked.

Zipporah must have been attractive. Moses had grown up in the Pharaoh's palace. He had spent his life sur-

63

rounded by beautiful women, and it was Zipporah, of all Jethro's seven daughters, whom he chose to be his wife.

"Besides that," she went on, stretching luxuriously on the soft grass beside the well, "being the wife of this peculiar man is not easy. I deserve credit, believe me. He is so strange sometimes, I think my nerves will break. It's as though my husband is with me in his body only. His thoughts are seldom here. And when I ask him what troubles him, he looks at me as though to tell me would be utter waste."

"Even I understand why Moses is troubled," Zipporah's youngest sister snapped. "He isn't really an Egyptian. He is a Hebrew. He was reared by the Pharaoh's daughter, but his thoughts are always with his own people back there in slavery to the Pharaoh. I don't feel one bit sorry for you, Zipporah. Moses is a great man. Only great men care about other people. Only great men carry great burdens on their minds. You're just too shallow to understand him!"

Moses had run away from Egypt, had fled for his life, after he murdered an Egyptian slave driver for mistreating a Hebrew slave, and although he found a home and a friend in old Jethro — even a wife in Zipporah — his heart had never come to rest in the country of the Midianites. He had named his first son Gershom because it meant "I have been a sojourner in a foreign land." He had found welcome with Jethro's household, but he could not forget his people back in Egypt.

The first real quarrel between Moses and Zipporah must have come at the birth of their child, Gershom. Of course, Moses wanted the boy circumcised according to the covenant of his Hebrew fathers. Evidently his father-in-law, Jethro, became a believer in the Lord God in his later years, (Exodus 18:10, 11) but there is no sign that Zipporah did. Gershom was not circumcised. And undoubtedly, Moses carried guilt over this omission. What

64

had begun happily with Zipporah may have begun to disintegrate at this point because after God commanded Moses to return to Egypt and free his people, even though Zipporah and their two sons, Gershom and Eliezer, went along, there is no indication that Moses' journey was peaceful. Of all times in his life, he needed a loyal wife on that journey. He was unsure of himself, frightened at the command of the Lord God.

And on the way, in an inn in a strange city, Moses fell mortally ill.

"Will our father die?" Gershom asked.

"He must not die," Zipporah said sharply. "What will happen to us in a strange place if he dies?"

But Moses was dying and she knew it.

"Why doesn't the Lord God heal him?" Gershom asked her.

Zipporah bit her lips, turning in her mind the one possibility for saving her husband. "He is probably angry with him, this Lord God your father worships! I did not permit you to be circumcised, Gershom. The Lord God is probably angry."

And not, apparently, out of faith, but out of fear that she would be left alone with two children in a strange city, Zipporah grabbed a knife and hacked away Gershom's foreskin herself. The boy lay screaming with pain as his mother took the bloody skin, rubbed Moses' feet with it, and cried hysterically: "Surely, you are a bridegroom of blood to me! Surely, you are a bridegroom of blood to me!"

* * * * * * * * * *

Moses got well, but I doubt that he recovered because poor, frustrated, inadequate Zipporah had pacified God. I do not see the Lord God, as He revealed Himself in Jesus Christ, as a God to pacify. God was going to heal Moses anyway. He had an enormous job for the man

65

to do. He needed Moses strong in his body as well as his mind and his spirit.

It does not seem to me that one needs to examine Zipporah's motives — they are too plain. Too plainly *mixed*. She lived, evidently in darkness, with no sense of God. And it is well to remember here that there is no reason to expect anything but selfish inadequacy from anyone who lives in darkness as Zipporah lived in it. Her emotions swung wildly one way and then another, as she battled with only her woman's wits to get her way with Moses.

If ever a man needed a wise, balanced, loyal wife to encourage him, Moses did. And as is so often true with great men (truer more often than women like to admit), he had an inadequate, neurotic, self-seeking, peevish wife. If ever a man had need of a strong helpmeet, Moses had — and he ended up with Zipporah.

I cannot condemn her any more than I can like her. I pity her, however, as much as I pity Moses, because apparently she wanted her marriage to work. She didn't know how to give it a chance, but she fought every step of the way. Her energies were misdirected, but she made the effort — a wrong effort in every instance, so far as the record tells — but an effort just the same.

The circumcision episode must have shown Moses there was no point in trying any longer. He sent her and the children back home to her father, Jethro, before they reached Egypt. There was too much ahead to have the nerve-stretching strain of an inadequate, helplessly neurotic wife tagging along. He knew she and the children would be safe with his beloved father-in-law, and so he sent them home.

66   Once Moses' mission was accomplished — once the children of Israel had been brought out of the land of Egypt — old Jethro brought Zipporah and the children to see Moses. There was no animosity in Moses' heart to-

ward her. Evidently, there was little or nothing there. He and Jethro greeted each other warmly; he listened as wise old Jethro gave him sound advice. Moses had exhausted himself attempting to handle all the personal problems of his people alone. Jethro could see his son-in-law was going to become ill from overwork, and so he suggested that his son-in-law appoint judges among the people to help him. Moses was humble enough to take Jethro's advice, but there is no indication at all that Zipporah entered into the picture in any way. In the narrative of the reunion of Moses with his family, she was there with the two boys, but only Moses and Jethro are written about. His wife had proven inadequate, and while he did not despise her, she had ceased to be a part of his life.

Perhaps if Moses had lived after Jesus Christ came, he would have been given light enough to find a way to help Zipporah. In the twilight era in which he obeyed God to the limits of his ability, he did not know how to do anything other than what he did.

Jesus has come now. The Holy Spirit is here to stay. Inadequate people can be made adequate — if they choose to be.

Deborah

...the woman adequate to everything

Deborah

...the woman adequate to everything

In the hill country of Ephraim, on the road between Ramah and Bethel, lived an amazing woman named Deborah. She was as rare among women as the palm tree in her front yard among trees in that part of Palestine. But Deborah — prophetess, poet, singer, wife, judge, patriot, military expert — had a royal palm tree in her yard, and under it, she held forth among the Israelites, counseling them, singing psalms to encourage their hearts toward the Lord God, making decisions, and taking actions which affected not only personal lives, but the national life of Israel itself.

Almost incidentally, Deborah was a housewife. Most writers imply (as though it were impolite not to, in view of her fantastic abilities otherwise) that Judge Deborah was an excellent, loving wife — a perfect homemaker — for her somewhat nondescript husband, Lappidoth. But her fame lay in the area of her wisdom, her brilliant mind, and her daring even in the planning and execution of guerrilla warfare.

For over twenty years, King Jabin, of the land of Canaan, had shown extreme cruelty to the children of

Israel, who, just after Moses' death, had come at last into their Promised Land. They were there, but not exactly being made welcome. Jabin saw to it that their women were dishonored, their vineyards — by one means or another — regularly damaged or destroyed. He had even begun to kill their children at play. Whether because of this maltreatment, feeling God had deserted them, or to please the king, many Israelites had turned to the worship of idols.

Where Judge Deborah lived, in the hills, life was safer than on the plains because the king's main power over them was the constant threat of extinction by his nine hundred iron chariots, capable of mass murder in the low country. In Deborah's hill country, the iron chariots were ineffective. They were too heavy to be drawn up the steep slopes, and so, there Israel was a bit more orderly, a bit more peaceful.

Day after day, when the oppressed Hebrews from the plains climbed to her front yard to counsel with her under her tall palm tree, Deborah would prod them to come alive against the oppression, to begin again to honor the Lord God who had led them out of Egypt. With all her great, intrepid heart, Deborah believed that if they would do this, God could again come to their rescue. This belief burned within her throughout every minute of every day and night. Over and over, she chided the men of Israel for being such cowards, for failing to provide leadership.

As generous as it may be to declare Deborah a delicate, feminine woman, she showed no indication of it. Men as well as women flocked to her tree to take of her inner strength and strong spirit. And when she began to see that some of her own enthusiasm for overwhelming their seemingly impossible enemy had begun to catch on, she decided to take the first step herself. No man had stepped forth to do it, but this did not stop Deborah.

72

From Kedesh, she summoned Barak, one of Israel's most astute military officers, and the first question she asked Barak was this: "Are you afraid of this man Sisera, the commander of King Jabin's army?"

"I am afraid of no single man, ma'am," Barak replied.

"Don't evade my question! Are you afraid of Sisera and his iron chariots?"

Barak was silent a moment, and then he grinned a little sheepishly. "I have thought of no way to defeat them."

This was all Deborah needed. She proceeded to give Barak a summary of the history of the nation of Israel, reminding him of how God had led them out of Egypt, across the Red Sea, breaking the hateful Pharaoh's hold on their very lives. "We are now *in* the Promised Land of Canaan, are we not, Barak?" And before he could answer, she went on, "Yes, we're here, but no one among us is acting as though he lives under the power of the Lord God of Israel. I am sick to death of cowering men. We will act. We will act decisively, and we will act now."

Barak began to brighten as he listened, his shoulders straightened, and Deborah knew she had managed to rekindle his faith. So, before he let it slip again, she declared: "It is not merely a woman who speaks to you. I, Deborah, am the prophetess of God. Does not the Lord, the God of Israel, command you, 'Go, gather your men at Mount Tabor, taking ten thousand from the tribe of Naphtali and the tribe of Zebulun'? 'And I will,' says the Lord God, 'draw out Sisera, the general of Jabin's army, to meet you by the river Kishon with his chariots and his troops; and I will give him into your hand.'"

For another long moment, Barak stood before Deborah in silence. "If you will go with me, I will go, but if you will not go with me, I will not go," he said at last.

73

"I will surely go with you, Barak." Deborah had evidently expected him to say that, and she kept her word.

Together, she and Barak called the men to arms, as she had ordered, and according to the promise God had given her, Sisera met them in battle.

For a moment, Barak must have held back, hesitated, because Deborah, as they faced the iron chariots, shouted: "Up! For this is the day in which the Lord has given Sisera into your hand. Does not the Lord go out before you, Barak?"

The Lord did go out before them, and in the midst of a downpour of rain which muddied the earth so that the heavy, lumbering iron chariots were bogged down, Barak and Deborah were victorious. Sisera, defeated and frightened for his life, fled on foot.

* * * * * * * * * *

No one in his right mind could doubt that Deborah, the judge, was an edequate woman — adequate to everything — even warfare. She was not only wise from a human point of view, she was strong. And perhaps right here, we should note that she did not use her human strength alone to accomplish what she saw needed to be done; she used her strong will, her iuner determination in order to enable her to lay hold of the very strength of the Lord God.

Deborah's faith was even stronger than her will.

I do not believe we are to chastise ourselves if we are not all, by nature, as resolute as Deborah. In fact, a world full of Deborahs might get a bit cumbersome at times. What I see that we can learn from this dramatic episode in the life of this unusual woman is this: She was a true prophetess. *A prophet or prophetess is merely a man or woman who can receive clear insights from God,* who can receive direction from God Himself without tainting or distorting it by his or her own ideas. Deborah was like this. She had a straight line to the Lord God, and she made use of it. For a woman with all of Deborah's many

74

talents, this is more difficult to do than for those of us who have fewer talents. Even on her own, Deborah would have been an outstanding woman, and so it is all the more amazing that she insisted upon giving God the credit for the impressive things she engineered.

Deborah lived before the Holy Spirit was available to live His life within the life of every believer. In her day, God enlightened the hearts and minds of those few whom He chose to be His prophets and prophetesses. Obviously, He had chosen Deborah, and I certainly am more impressed when a ten-talent woman can hear God as a child hears its parent's voice. Deborah is one of my favorite women in the entire Bible for this reason. I admire her far more for being simple and trusting with the Lord God than for her many abilities and her courage.

She was particularly chosen of God to give His words to the struggling, rebellious Hebrew children. But she was no more particularly chosen then than all Christian women are chosen now. The Holy Spirit is abroad in our struggling, rebellious world — available to you and to me. Women can now receive insight from God — direct. Of course, happily, we always have the Bible to keep us from going overboard on our insights — especially do I find the Gospels of value here — but we women who live in the twentieth century can, in a definite sense, be prophetesses too. I think God expects it of us. No more than He expects men to be prophets, of course, because His Holy Spirit is for everyone. But the one, simple point I think we need to see here in the story of Deborah is that insight from God is possible for us all now that Jesus has come.

Having a straight line to the Father does not make us superior spiritually. And I know there are some who, by nature, seem to have more spiritual sensitivity than others. To deny this would be false. But because Pentecost has happened, anyone with a reasonably normal mind can

75

get enough insight from God to live an adequate life. We won't all be adequate to everything, as Deborah seemed to be, but we can be adequate to meet what life demands of us in the areas of our relationships — if we stay open to God.

Delilah

...the beautiful trickster

Delilah

...the beautiful trickster

Samson, the most powerful man in all Judah, was more than a physical giant; he was a judge of the people, respected, revered by many because of his wisdom as well as his superhuman strength. Single-handed, he had killed a lion, and when his own people bound him with thick ropes to deliver him as a political trophy to their enemies, the Philistines, Samson shook himself and snapped the ropes as though they had been twine. With nothing more than the jawbone of a donkey, the big man had killed hundreds of Philistines in the midst of their search for him. Over and over they had attacked Samson's people, the Israelites, and over and over he foiled their efforts.

A Nazarite, dedicated to the Lord's service from birth, he kept his Nazarite vows faithfully — never shaving, never drinking fermented liquor, never cutting his hair — so that the very strength of God flowed through him. To capture Samson became a national emergency among the Philistines. Military might and iron bonds could not hold him. He had once uprooted two iron door posts and crumpled a city gate. A method must be found to deplete his enormous energy, to weaken him.

79

In spite of his success as a judge, and in spite of his supernatural strength, Samson had a weakness about which everyone knew: He loved beautiful women. The times were primitive, and quite casually the Biblical account speaks of his stopping off at the houses of beautiful harlots. Samson kept his Nazarite vows where his hair, his beard, and his sobriety were concerned, but he was drunk often on his passion for the bodies of the women who attracted him. Evidently the Nazarite vows did not cover this discipline, and Samson fell into the Philistine trap. A seductively beautiful "trap" named Delilah, who had been offered eleven hundred pieces of silver from each Philistine lord if she could discover the secret of Samson's strength so that he could be brought down.

"Delilah, I have known many women, but I have never loved anyone but you." He pulled her toward him on the silk covered pile of rugs in the corner of her comfortable house. "I love you, Delilah!"

When she could free herself, she laughed, and pain creased Samson's broad, bearded face. "Why do you laugh at me?" he demanded.

"I'm not really laughing at you, dear Samson. I'm puzzled. Puzzled that you could think you really love me more than the others."

"I puzzle you, Delilah? My heart is as open toward you as the heart of a shepherd boy!"

She stood up. "It's my womanly curiosity, Samson. You are so magnificent — I must know if anything could bind you so that you would be like other men. If you really loved me, you would tell me."

Samson laughed. "Is that all? I'll gladly tell you how I can be reduced to the weakness of other men. If you would have me bound with seven fresh wood fiber cords — still green and strong, not yet dried — then I shall become weak like any other man."

Delilah clapped her hands, and a Philistine prince, who

80

had been hiding behind the draperies in her room, brought the fresh wood fiber cords as soon as they could be secured. Delilah herself tied the laughing Samson securely, stepped back, and cried: "The Philistines are upon you, Samson! Save yourself!"

Samson, too much in love to consider her treachery, enjoying the little game, shook himself, snapped the tough bonds, and reached laughingly for Delilah.

When she once more begged to know the secret of his great strength, Samson went on playing his game with her. This time he broke out of a heavy bind of new, unused rope as though it were dried vines.

Delilah laughed with him, pretending she, too, was merely playing a lover's game, but she was far from finished. Each Philistine lord standing behind her draperies had promised her eleven hundred silver pieces, and Delilah loved money more than she could ever have loved a man.

Samson's visits grew more frequent simply because he was powerless to stay away from her. She filled his horizons; he thought of almost nothing else but the scent of her perfume, the firm, young arms slipped about his neck, the slender fingers moving through his long, thick hair.

"Samson, you have made a fool of me with your lies and your games. How can you pretend to love me?" Her face was close to his, and her breath was like flowers. His deep eyes laughed beneath his thick brows, but Delilah was frowning.

"This time, beloved Delilah, I will tell you the truth. Weave my hair into that cloth you're weaving there on your loom, and I'll be as helpless as a little fish."

There was no need this time to signal the Philistine lords. She knew they were waiting behind the heavy curtains. Feeling he had told her the truth at last, she pretended not to hurry now. She kissed Samson and cradled his big head on her shoulder until he fell asleep.

81

While he slept, she deftly wove the locks of thick, brown hair into the cloth on her loom. Her shrill cry woke him with a start: "Samson! The Philistines are upon you!"

He jumped to his feet, tearing loose the pin from the loom along with the cloth. Delilah leaped at him in fury, thought better of it, and fell into his arms. Having her there was all of life to him. Reason drained from the great and mighty judge of Judah. He forgot even the Lord his God and blurted his secret to the woman who had done what a thousand Philistines had not been able to do.

"Oh, my Delilah, I'll tell you the secret of my strength. I did not know it meant so much to you. I love you, Delilah, and to prove it I will end the games. I will tell you the whole secret. My strength is from God. I am a Nazarite from my mother's womb. I have vowed never to cut my hair. If I do, I lose God's strength at once. If a razor ever touches my head, I will be weak like any other man."

Delilah signaled no one. This time she would be as careful with him as she knew how to be. Nothing must go wrong. Her woman's instinct told her she had discovered the truth at last. As the Philistine lords watched from behind their curtains, she stayed close to Samson, caressing his massive head with her jeweled hands, vowing her love for him. And once more, after he had vented his passion, she lulled him to sleep with tender words and soft kisses on his long hair. When he was sleeping soundly, she signaled the lords and the razors flashed.

As soon as the last lock was gone, Delilah could feel the strength leave Samson's big arms and shoulders. Even she could control him now.

82   * * * * * * * * * *

Delilah, of course, is always considered one of the most wicked, heartless women in the Bible. Nineteenth century writers commenting on her colorful story explode with caustic phrases about her evil heart, her immorality, her love of "filthy lucre." They are right. Delilah was everything the Book of Proverbs says a woman should not be.

And yet, I doubt that women today — at least those who might be reading or studying this book in a women's group — can be helped much by such defamation of Delilah. She was "treacherous," "infamous," "vile," but there is a subtle danger here for us: When we skim over the story of Delilah's treachery, feeling removed from it in our own lives, being convinced it has little or nothing to do with us, we make a serious mistake.

We may not be harlots, or even overtly conniving and deceitful as Delilah was, but many of us *are* deceitful. Subtly so, of course, or so we hope, but deceitful nonetheless. In fact, I think all of us have streaks of deception, and if my mail and many-remembered conversations are any criterion, there are wives today who are as mercilessly deceitful, as doggedly tricky with their husbands, as Delilah was with Samson.

These outwardly "moral" women do not necessarily use sexual devices (although some do), but deceit is deceit — trickery is trickery — and in my opinion, this was Delilah's sin. Again, we have to remember that the culture, the social and spiritual mores of Samson's time were different from ours. The Bible does quite casually mention that "Samson went to Gaza, and there he saw a harlot, and he went in to her" (Judges 16:1). And then the account goes right on to another subject. So, Delilah's example for us is perhaps more her deceit than her overt immorality. And here we need to be honest with ourselves.

What are some of the ways in which today's woman can show the same deadly deception in her relationships with her husband? She can, as we have already said, 83 practice seduction of her mate in order to get something she wants. She can, and often does, build him up to his face and then tear him down before her friends — ordinarily, as a way of drawing sympathy to herself. "Oh, I wouldn't let my husband know I think this for anything in the world — I tell him he's the best accountant in his office — but I know he really isn't. He'd have had a raise long ago if he were!" "I keep telling my husband he isn't looking a bit middle-aged, but I don't need to tell you he is. Makes me sad sometimes when I think how good his waistline used to be. I never imagined myself being married to a paunchy male, but I am. Only, I wouldn't have him know that I told *you!*"

Other women systematically practice deceit by criticizing a man before his children, by turning the children against their father when he isn't at home to defend himself. "I never say anything in front of *him,* but now and then when the children and I are alone, I feel I must set them straight about certain of their father's weaknesses. Some day I may need them to take my side against him."

"What do I do when I want a new outfit and my husband says we can't afford it? I cry. I just cry my heart out. He can't stand to see a woman cry."

As surely as Delilah used her razor, these women are using theirs.

Our "razors" are called womanly wiles, womanly wits, womanly deceit, coquetry, and other "acceptable" names, but in each instance, a woman has hunted until she found a man's weak spot, and then she takes over. This is, in a very definite sense, playing God in another person's life. Only God deserves to control human life. Only God is capable of doing it without destruction.

As did Delilah in Samson's time, the "Delilahs" now are reverting to type — Mother Eve's type. The first woman wanted to be "in control," and so she grabbed the forbidden fruit, knew her husband's weakness for fruit, tempted him into eating it too, and our trouble began.

The Biblical Delilah was a primitive woman, but she is still alive in us — to one extent or another.

84

Ichabod's mother

...all sorrow and despair

Ichabod's mother

...all sorrow and despair

In the bloody battle between the Philistines, encamped at Aphek, and the Israelites, encamped at Ebenezer, four thousand Israelites had been killed, and the "armies of the Lord" were routed. Back in their camp at Ebenezer the troubled army elders of Israel demanded to know why the Lord had not given them victory against their long despised enemies.

After long consultation, in a desperate effort to put down the Philistines, the elders decided to send men to the temple at Shiloh, where blind, aging Eli was priest. The men were instructed to carry the ark of the Lord out of the temple and onto the battlefield. They had known nothing but defeat. Perhaps, they figured, if they could have the presence of the Lord in the covenant ark with them, they could win.

Eli was old and weakened in his spirit, so it was no trick at all to talk him into releasing the ark. His two sons, Hophni and Phinehas, were to be guardians of the ark during the upcoming battle. There was more religious superstition abroad among the Israelites at that period in their history than faith in the living God. Only Eli and

87

his daughter-in-law, the devout wife of Phinehas, feared for the ark of the Lord.

"It is not right, daughter," Eli said to her after his two sons had hurried out of sight, the ark on their shoulders. "It is wrong to remove the ark from the temple of God."

"I know it is, my father," the young woman replied, wringing her hands. "Some dreadful tragedy will come upon us all because of it. I'm afraid! I'm always so afraid when I do not know just where the ark is."

The old man's cheeks were wet with tears as his set, sightless eyes stared blankly in the direction of the fearful young woman. "Take me to the roadside, daughter, and prepare a place for me that I might watch — or at least be nearby — when and if they return carrying the blessed ark."

His daughter-in-law had just left him, seated at the side of the road over which the soldiers would travel on their return, when the pains began to come. She was nearly ready to bear Phinehas their first child, and she hurried as fast as she was able back to her tent before it was too late. Someone will bring me news of the battle, she thought, as she sank onto her bed in hard labor.

"Someone will surely bring me news of the battle — and the blessed ark of the Lord," she gasped between the wracking pains. The midwife answered, trying to reassure her, but the fear never left her eyes.

Perhaps because the Philistines feared the presence of the ark in the Israelite camp, they fought harder than ever — with more brutality, more energy, more determination to smash their Hebrew enemies once and for all. Word reached old Eli sitting at the side of the road, by the first group of fleeing, defeated Israelite soldiers. "This time we were really beaten, old man," they shouted. "Not four thousand of our number fell, but thirty thousand."

"Thirty thousand!" Eli gasped.

"Your two sons among them, sir, and the ark has been stolen!"

The old man reeled on his chair, lost his balance, and tipped over, breaking his neck. He had intended to be led to the tent of his daughter-in-law, to comfort her in her birth pain, but he died within minutes and never saw her again.

"Did anyone tell my father-in-law, Eli, that his sons are dead?" Phinehas' wife whispered when she heard about the latest battle.

"Yes," replied the gossip who had burst into her tent with the news. "The old man was told, and it killed him too!"

The pain ridden young woman stared at the black side wall of her goatskin tent. "It — killed — him?" And then she sighed. "No, the death of his two worthless sons did not kill the old priest Eli."

"Well," the news-bearer insisted, "the old man toppled right off his chair — dead as a stone."

"I do not doubt that he's dead, but it was the news of the ark that killed him." Her face contorted with physical and spiritual pain. She clutched the covers on her bed and screamed.

The baby was born, but there was no joy in its mother's eyes.

"Fear not," the midwife comforted her, "for you have borne a son."

The exhausted young woman said nothing.

"You must not despair," the nurse repeated. "Your husband is dead, but you have borne a son."

She still stared vacantly at the tent wall, tears running down her pale cheeks. "I — will — name — my poor son — Ichabod," she whispered almost lifelessly. "For the glory has departed from Israel. My husband did not love me. I lived only for the Lord God. My husband was a bad man — an — evil — man. He lay often — with — the women — who served — at the temple gate. I had no hope in — the love of — my husband. Now he is — dead. His brother — is dead. My father-in-law Eli who — loved God — is also dead." She was scarcely breathing at all, and her hand hung limply over the side of her bed. "I — I will — name my poor, hopeless — son, Ichabod, because — the glory has — departed — from all Israel. For — the ark of God has been — captured. There is — no hope left — anywhere."

The young woman gasped weakly; her head rolled to one side. She was dead.

* * * * * * * * * *

This very sad story is its own commentary. The nameless young woman lost all hope and died. Her life had been almost complete tragedy. Her husband did not love her and was steadily unfaithful, so that the years of her married life had been an agony of uncertainty. Only her father-in-law had been her friend, and now he was dead too.

Some will ask if the responsibility of caring for a newborn baby should not have been enough to give her a will to live. Well, it wasn't. Whether it should have or not is really beside the point. Hope can die for each of us at different crisis points in our lives. What might strengthen one woman would weaken another. Somehow it is very easy for me to understand this young mother. Having the new baby to rear alone was the breaking point for her, not the point of strength.

Others may wonder about her faith in the Lord God. Wasn't that enough to give her a desire to live? *Shouldn't her faith have given her strength?* Well, it didn't. And it occurs to me that the reason it didn't is that, like so many women today, her faith was more sentimental superstition than faith. Her spiritual life collapsed when the ark was captured. Her faith was in the ark, not in the living Lord.

90

Her faith must have been in the way the ark made her *feel*. If our faith is in our emotional responses to the God of love, instead of in the God of love Himself, it will not hold us during our crisis times, either. It isn't that God isn't always willing to hold us. It is that we have had our faith in the "ark" of our feeling, in a symbol, in a particular church, in a prayer group, in a Christian leader — in a religious experience. These are all subject to change. None will hold us when the blows fall. Only God can do this.

Most of us have never known complete despair — total hopelessness. This woman did, and she drowned in it without a fight. We cannot condemn her. Some of us who perhaps do not even understand how anyone could be totally without hope may find out one day. Tragedy can fall on anyone. It is urgent that well ahead of time we find the one Rock on which we dare fasten our hope. Not things about God, not rituals, not even the Scriptures alone, but the living person of Jesus Christ, who promised that He would be with us always.

Michal

…David's insensitive wife

...David's insensitive wife

Michal, aging, her once beautiful face drawn with the
bitterness she had carried in her heart for most of the
years of her tragic life, sat alone in her room in David's
palace. She was still his wife but she had borne him no
children, and because of the estrangement between them
— an estrangement she had never understood — her days
and nights were spent alone. Even her five nephews, the
sons of her dead sister Merab, were gone now — all be-
headed.

"I resented those five sons of my dead sister, but at
least they were my charges. Now, there is no one."

In her loneliness, Michal often spoke aloud to herself,
still trying — sometimes almost desperately — to discover
why her life, which had begun so romantically and with
such high promise, should have ended as it was ending.
Propped on the pile of silken pillows in her palace room,
she would go back over the years, savoring the beautiful
days, trying to blot out the ugly ones. Always she failed
in her attempt to understand how it had all turned so
sour. And yet, she had only her handmaidens to talk to
if she didn't talk to herself, and more and more often,
Michal chose herself.

95

"I have not laid eyes on my husband, David the king, in over a month — and then from a distance, as he hobbled through the palace garden with that woman — his favorite wife — Bathsheba. Hm! Bathsheba. How, even as an old woman, does she still have such a hold on the King? Not that I care," Michal lied to herself. "After all, I was his first wife — his first choice. And even after I grew bored with his long absence and married poor Palti who loved me so tenderly, King David did not forget me."

At this point in her reminiscing, Michal would sigh heavily and smile a little. "Poor Palti, how he loved me! I can still hear his weeping as he followed after me the day the King sent for me to return to him at his palace. A grown man, Palti, strong in battle, intelligent — weeping as a child weeps because he was losing me forever." Here, Michal's smile would vanish and the deep furrow would crease her old forehead again. "Why did David send for me after all those years as another man's wife? Was it because he knew in our youth, in the early days of our marriage, I had saved his life? After all, it was I who let him down from our bedroom window so that he might escape my father Saul's wrath. It was I who put an image in his bed and covered it with a sleeping cloth to fool my father's messengers who had come to slay him. How my father hated David!" Her smile would return here, remembering King David as a young man. "The most beautiful body a man ever had," she whispered. "The straightest legs, the widest shoulders — and that head — noble, heavy with red-gold curls. How I desired him! How I loved the young David! So much did I love him that the day my insane father tried to kill him with his own spear as my David sang for him with his heavenly voice, I felt my own breath would be cut off if his life were taken. The very sight of young, courageous David was reason enough for me to wake up in the mornings — to have him as my husband was my whole life."

96

Struggling off her pallet, Michal would — every time she reached this point in her remembering — hurry as fast as her stiff old legs would take her to the tiny, high window. At this point the room always became too small and so stuffy she found breathing difficult, her loneliness so acute she had to speak aloud: "I loved him. I desired him. I saved his life once — and now I despise him!" Her faded eyes scanned the clouds in the sky as though searching there for the answer to why she now despised the King. And then she would sink again in her bed. "The question is not why do I despise him, but why does he now despise me? I did nothing any self-respecting wife would not have done. There he was dancing half-naked in the streets with those common servant girls! So, he had brought the ark of the Lord back — what was so wonderful about that? He was always a fool about that ark, and so long as he didn't humiliate me, I didn't complain that he took his religion so seriously. But that day, when he acted up like a boor in a public street, laughing and dancing and praising his God with those common people — well, any decent, self-respecting wife with an ounce of pride would have complained. Why, I could scarcely believe my eyes when I looked out the window and saw him acting as any rough working man would act. I despised him in my heart as I watched him! And when he had finished his orgy with the peasants in the street, he had the nerve to come home as though he had done nothing at all. I ran out to meet him, unable to restrain myself — so angry I could have choked. 'How the king of Israel honored himself today,' I shouted, 'uncovering himself before the eyes of his servants' maids, as one of the vulgar fellows shamelessly uncovers himself!' And then he had the gall to say he was dancing before the Lord who had chosen *him* to be king over my father, Saul — and to rub salt in my wounds by informing me that those

97

common maid servants understood him because they worshiped his God too!"

She shuddered at the memory — shuddered and turned her thoughts immediately away. She had lost David *that day,* and she knew it. He had never come in to lie with her again, so that "she had no child to the day of her death."

* * * * * * * * * *

I have thought a long time about Michal. What was she really like? Of course, the Old Testament's somewhat sketchy narration leaves the filling in of character traits and personality quirks somewhat to our imaginations, our psychological and spiritual perceptions. Unlike some of the other women of David's time, Michal apparently did nothing that would shock even the "civilized" twentieth century moralist. At least, there is no account of Michal's having been an adulteress. She seems to have been duly married to both David and Palti. Of course, when she left the grieving Palti to return to David, she had no choice. According to the custom of her time, when a king asked for a woman, he got her no matter what her marital status.* King David sat on the throne after the death of Saul, he wanted Michal back, and back she went. Did you ever wonder if she wanted to go back to David after all those years away? To me, it is quite possible that she had lost interest in him — that his long absence (while he stayed out of the insane Saul's reach) made Michal's heart grow fonder of someone else, her loving, devoted second husband, Palti. There is no way of knowing this, but one thing seems sure — Michal was in the dark about herself. Most likely she conformed outwardly to the religion of David and her father, Saul, but there is no doubt that Michal's inner-light was dim or non-existent. Self-understanding seems impossible without the light of some form of inner contact with the Lord God. Michal's values

98

* See the next chapter on another wife of David's, Bathsheba.

were almost certainly worldly. Like many "professing Christians" today, she cared more for social status, the family image in the eyes of the servants, and the power that would come to her if she left Palti and went back to David, who had become the king. Of course, there is no reason to think her hard-hearted. I feel certain she experienced a wrench as Palti wept along behind her, following her as far as possible, as she left him. But she went, and her personal reasons for going were probably many. One of them was the love of prestige; another may have been some sort of lingering love for David.

After all, he had been promised her sister, Merab, first, and if it hadn't been for Saul's trickery in giving his daughter, Merab, to another man, David would have married her. Saul did give Merab away, though, and here we have the key to Michal's deep fascination with David: ". . . Saul's daughter, Michal, loved David." The Scriptures are explicit about this. She apparently talked often about how much she wanted to marry the brave, handsome shepherd because we read that, ". . . they told Saul, and the thing pleased him." The issue is not that Saul's delight came from his hope that if he could get David to "fight the battles of the Lord" for him in order to gain Michal's hand, the young man might be killed. Saul's hatred here is not the issue, except that Michal wanted David in spite of her own father's dislike of him. The issue here is that Michal had set her heart on David. At least, she felt an enormous physical attraction to him. She was "in love," as we say, and determined to have him.

So, when she first married David, she loved him — to the extent of her capacity to love. As I have grown older, I have come to see more and more the wide difference between loving (agape) and being in love (eros). They can happen together, but sooner or later love (agape) has to take over: Love that concerns itself first of all with the welfare of the loved one and ceases to worry about

99

itself. I don't believe for a minute that poor Michal *loved* David. Not in the sense that what mattered to him was more important than what mattered to her.

This, quite inevitably, left her in darkness — not only about his true nature, but about her own. Somehow I feel quite sure that even as an old woman, Michal was still trying to figure out how her life had gone so wrong when it had begun so well. She had returned to David when he called for her, but the years had withered some of her passion for him. She had become what should be recognizable to us — a rather average, insensitive wife. Perhaps when she first came back to David, she was still attractive, but the glow had faded from whatever had sparkled her old love for him. She may have gone back to David much as one who has been far away from an adolescent love attempts to "go back again." There are, of course, happy reunions like this, even marriages, but usually one finds the spark quite dead. This may have happened to Michal, and if so, all she had left then was the honor of being the king's wife, the ease and respectability of life in the palace. These apparently filled her life because the minute David, in his childlike exuberance over the return of the ark of the Lord, embarrassed her, she flew at him like a furious hen.

Undoubtedly, what love David had left for Michal died during that vindictive speech in which she said in effect: "You certainly made a spectacle of yourself today! How do you dare embarrass me this way in front of the neighbors and the palace servants? What will people think?"

Michal did not know David's God — not personally — and because she didn't, we cannot condemn her. Her own inner poverty of spirit limited her vision. The servant girls with whom David danced for joy as he worshiped the Lord, his God, understood. They knew and loved the same God David loved. Michal was in the dark — watching them make spectacles of themselves —

100

hatred for her husband growing in her heart as she watched. Real love cannot turn to hatred. Real love cannot despise, even when it does not understand. David lost his charm for her when he did something that she could not understand. His love for the God of his fathers was anathema to her. She simply saw no point in it — certainly not for a king. And obviously, at that moment, the attraction they both felt for each other vanished like an April snowflake.

Never in a million years would Michal have understood what Paul meant when he said we are to be "fools for Christ's sake" (I Corinthians 4:10). David would have known at once. He loved the Lord God with that same reckless, foolhardy simplicity. Michal did not, and so David embarrassed her.

She is sadly typical of many women today who love their husbands only to the extent of shared experience. Of course, the safe way for any marriage — as for any human relationship — is the shared experience of God. We can disagree on any number of other things and keep on loving, if we agree about God.

Bathsheba

...acting on forgiveness

Bathsheba

...acting on forgiveness

Down the narrow, winding road that led from Jerusalem, Bathsheba walked with the people — a little apart, since she was King David's favorite wife, but this day she would not remain within the safety and comfort of the palace. She could not stay away from what was about to happen. Her son Solomon, the most loved of her four living sons by David, astride his father's mule, was on his way to be made king.

She took a deep breath of the fresh, spring air as she walked briskly in the procession that wound its way from Jerusalem toward the Gihon Spring in the valley below. It was such a day as this, Bathsheba thought, that King David first saw me bathing on the roof of my house. A frown crossed her still beautiful face. A spring day such as this when all my life was turned around, changed, sent in a direction I would never have dreamed. King David. When he had first sent for her that day so long ago, she had to go. A mere woman, the lowliest subject of a mighty king, had no choice but to obey. Before God, she had confessed that going to the king had not been unpleasant for her. She was young, and King David so powerful and

105

handsome, any woman would have gone. At least, Bathsheba had comforted herself in her guilt by believing any woman would have obeyed his command to love him. Did he know, she had wondered many times, that her husband Uriah — her good and loyal husband Uriah — was at war in the king's own army? Did King David know she was alone? Or would he have sent for her just the same? She had never asked. There had seemed no reason to ask. Things had happened so swiftly. "I am with child," she had told him. Just that and nothing more. She wanted no comfort, no way out of her predicament unless the king wanted to help her. It must be what *he* desires for me, she decided, and so asked no favors. She would bear the scandal, and there would be a scandal. Her husband had been gone too long for anyone to believe the child she carried was Uriah's child.

The crowd of people began to sing softly up ahead as the priestly procession followed her son, Solomon, to the place of the anointing. Bathsheba did not join the singing. Her thoughts were too much for singing. This king, this sensitive, once self-gratifying, utterly human King David had come to her rescue; had tried tricking Uriah into making love to her during a leave from battle, and when Uriah had refused to break his vow not to touch a woman until the war was over, David had seen to it that Uriah was killed in the next battle. A noble king? No. Not always noble. Sometimes, yes. But human first, and hers — hers in a way he had never been with his other wives. If it had been mere lust that brought them together the first time, their hearts had become one as they shared the bitter grief at the death of that first child. And now, their favorite of the other four sons, Solomon, was going to be king because his father had kept a vow to her.

They had reached the Gihon Spring, and Solomon had been helped from the royal mule. The great crowd of people was silent, watching expectantly, reverent in the

106

presence of the Lord God, as David's royal guard, the Cherethite and Pelethite men, stood in formation around the young son of her heart, as Zadok the priest, Nathan the prophet, and Benaiah, the son of Jehoiada, began their preparation for the anointing.

Nathan the prophet. Bathsheba's heart tightened for a moment, remembering the torment of guilt King David had experienced when Nathan, the prophet of God, had accused him of his sin with her. After a decent time of mourning for her dead husband, she had moved into the palace as David's wife, but days passed without a sight of him. She smiled. During that time he had made his peace with God, and with his peace, he had strengthened her own. Tears sprang to her eyes. David would not be with her long. He was old now. She and Nathan had been forced to remind him of his promise to make her son, Solomon, king of Israel in his place. David was old and forgetful, but he still loved her. The promise was carried out as soon as they had reminded him of it.

The priest Zadok was holding the horn of oil now, and in a moment, her son would be king. Still, memories crowded her mind. Bathsheba was growing old too; for her the past was an inseparable part of today.

She and Nathan had planned it all, had decided that she would go to the king first and prod his aging mind. He had looked so small and frail and weary propped on his bed, his once broad shoulders slumped against the pillows. Abishag, the Shunammite, was ministering to him. Bathsheba bowed that day and did obeisance, and in a thin, cracking voice, still warm with caring, David had asked: "What do you desire?"

"My lord," she said urgently, "you swore to your maid-servant by the Lord your God, saying, 'Solomon your son shall reign after me, and he shall sit upon my throne.' And now, behold, Adonijah is king, although you, my lord the king, do not know it." 107

She knew Adonijah, David's son by another wife, Haggith, had simply taken over, supported by his own court followers. Bathsheba had been forced to act. And faithful Nathan, keeping his promise, had joined them, urging the king to appoint Solomon to rule after him. According to custom, Bathsheba had left the king's chamber, but soon Nathan came out to her and told her the good news. "He has said, 'Call Bathsheba to me.' "

Here now, by Gihon Spring, the promise was being kept. Zadok, the priest, had almost finished his chant of holy words, any minute the oil would be running down over the beautiful head of her son, Solomon, and he would be king of Israel.

"May my lord King David live forever," Bathsheba breathed, and the air was split with the blast of the trumpet and the shouts of the people: "Long live King Solomon!"

Tears of joy streamed down Bathsheba's face as she whispered, "Yes, long live my son, King Solomon!"

* * * * * * * * * *

So much has been written about the weakness of David as he indulged himself in the sinful relationship with Bathsheba. Some choose to leave her mainly blameless, since it was true that any subject was obliged to obey the king. In my opinion, scholarly comments are almost irrelevant where David's guilt is concerned. Irrelevant, too, in relation to his sin. As my dear friend, Dr. Anna Mow, has said, the wonder is not the sin that David committed; the wonder is that in this primitive time — so long before Christ came — any man should have had a conscience sensitive enough to God to realize that he needed forgiveness. David not only realized that he had sinned, but his relationship with God was vital enough so that he recognized that his sin was against the Lord Himself. "Against thee, thee only, have I sinned" (Psalm 51). And,

108

as Nathan had pointed the finger of conviction at David, so had the old prophet of God assured the king of forgiveness: "The Lord also has put away your sin."

David knew God well enough to be able to *take* His forgiveness. We need to think on this. Christ had not yet come. Only a few men, mainly the prophets of God, who received direct revelations from Him grasped the meaning of forgiveness. David, "a man after God's own heart," following the first agony of his guilt, *took* forgiveness.

But we are considering Bathsheba and what God might have to say to us today through her dramatic story. Did she, too, experience guilt before God? Did she, too, repent and accept forgiveness?

I have no doubt at all that she did both. Guilt is a necessary part of repentance and forgiveness. Unless we know we need to be forgiven, we don't bother to ask for it or to receive it. And the reason for my certainty that Bathsheba must have shared an experience similar to David's is that David's own walk with God *after* his sin with her was stronger and more vital than ever. It makes no sense at all to think that this spiritually sensitive man would have continued to love and respect Bathsheba had she not entered also into the cleansing, re-creative forgiveness of the Lord God.

She was not David's only wife. He must have cared for some of the others, too, because he grieved deeply over the death of Absalom, his son by Maacah. Still, when he was an old man, nearing the end of his marvelous life, it was Bathsheba's son whom he chose to sit upon his throne as king of his beloved Israel. And it was Bathsheba whose request was granted, not the request of another wife. David must have respected her, trusted her judgment, and loved her more than the others.

It is true that she was beautiful, but women lose some of their dramatic beauty as they grow older, and Bathsheba was not young when Solomon was anointed king. Her beauty had turned inward, and a woman's inner beauty is almost always dependent upon her relationship with God.

With all my heart, I believe Bathsheba permitted God to do what He always longs to do for us all in the mysterious but totally creative and re-creative process of forgiveness: She permitted Him to strengthen and beautify her inner life, so that none of the sin — flagrant as it was — was a waste. Not because sin isn't destructive, but because she, like David, gave the sin to God and permitted Him to forgive it as He redeemed her.

More than that, Bathsheba forgave herself and went on to become a good mother, a faithful helpmeet to David, and a woman whose judgment even Nathan the prophet could admire and respect. This, I feel, is the big word God has for us as women today: *We need to accept forgiveness.* Too often we refuse, out of a kind of exalted and morbid self-concern, to forgive ourselves. We say we believe God has put our sin behind Him, but we don't do as much for ourselves. And in refusing to forgive ourselves, in continuing to chew over the old sins, we minimize, in an authentically blasphemous way, the very forgiveness of God Himself. If we have not forgiven ourselves — if we go on rehashing our sins, carrying the guilt — we have not really accepted the forgiveness of God. He never forces us. He always offers. Our part is to receive and to begin to act and to live in the all new, free, wide realm of forgiving love.

Bathsheba did this. And don't forget, the God whose ability to redeem is unlimited, permitted Bathsheba's name to appear in the genealogy of Jesus Christ.

Queen of Sheba

...wise woman with a hungry heart

Queen of Sheba

...wise woman with a hungry heart

The long, winding caravan of camels, their polished silver trappings gleaming in the sun, had moved for weeks across the wind-swept sands of the Arabian Desert. Five hundred of the more than one thousand miles lay behind her, and the young, handsome Queen of Sheba rode erect on her royal camel, uncomplaining of the sometimes sickening heat, more unmindful of the blowing sand, the drying sun than her camel drivers who walked along beside the great beasts. Her skin had to be oiled many times a day to prevent burning and cracking, and now and then she would dismount for exercise and massage. The long trip would not weary her; she would see to that. If it required all the energy of her fine mind, she would use it so that she could arrive at the court of the great King Solomon fresh, alert, ready to hear and absorb his famed wisdom. She had heard that Solomon of Israel was the wisest man in the world, and the richest. The Queen had glimpsed some of his wealth. From her palace on the Red Sea, she had seen his fine ships pass, laden, she was told, with pearls, emeralds, rare woods, and ivory. Solomon's caravans, carrying spices, perfumes, gold, and silver,

113

were the longest and the richest of all those that moved
through her land — their tributes paid to her, the most
costly.

Riches impressed her, although her land of Arabia was
mostly sandy wasteland. She ruled over few subjects,
but because all trade routes by land or sea went through
her country, she had become a powerful ruler. Sheba
was going to visit King Solomon to negotiate a new trade
treaty with him, but this was not her main reason.

"I'm going," she told her weary, complaining hand-
maiden, "because I have to go. That's reason enough. I
know how tired you are. I'm tired too, but this will not
cause us to turn back. Here, use some of my fine oil
on your face. It will help. And don't let me hear one
more complaint, because nothing is going to stop me from
discovering the mystery of the wisdom of King Solomon!
They tell me his wisdom comes from the God of Israel.
Well, I intend to find out about this God. I intend to
question the king as he's never been questioned before.
He may just meet his match in me."

Over the last stretches of the Arabian Desert and across
the land of Moab, the Queen's caravan moved until, after
a journey of almost twelve hundred miles, she glimpsed
the gold of Solomon's magnificent temple.

"I'm here," she murmured to no one in particular, as
she sat forward on the big animal, straining to see the
splendor that lay ahead. "I'm here, and I intend to stay
until my mind and my heart are imbued with the wisdom
that has made this man so great. I will test him with
riddles; I will ply him with every perplexing question at
my command. He will never have encountered a woman
so interested in his mind as I." She smiled to herself. "He
114   is a king rich in wives and concubines, but he has never
met the likes of me. Move those camels along! We are
there. We have come to the palace of the great King
Solomon."

Everything impressed her — even the dress of the low-liest servants in the court of Israel. And, although she accepted the lavish hospitality of the king himself, she also busied herself studying how the servants' garments were made. Her servants must have them, too, when she returned to her own land. With a quick and practiced eye, she made mental notes of the elegant clothing worn by Solomon's wives and concubines. Accustomed to the most lavish gowns herself, these challenged her. Day after day she toured the kingdom, speechless at times at its splendor. And at last, when she had made a careful survey of the physical beauty of the palace and all its appointments, she turned one morning to the king himself.

"I had heard about your kingdom, Sire, but the half was not told to me! I am speechless. How happy your wives must be. How happy the people over whom you rule."

Solomon bowed.

"And you, Sire," the Queen said smiling wisely, "you are as splendid as your kingdom." She raised her hand quickly. "Don't thank me. I am not complimenting you. I am merely stating a fact. Now that I have inspected your court and palace and warehouses, I must turn to the king."

"The king is honored," Solomon said. "He has never met a woman with your inquisitive mind. He has never met a woman with a mind honed to the sharp edge he observes in yours. Whatever you want to know, you will be told."

Hour upon hour the two sat together talking, or walked, deep in conversation, about the palace grounds, the Queen of Sheba plying him with all the questions she had kept so long unanswered in her heart. Their talk must have ranged from the Lord God at creation all the way to life after death, and Sheba listened, breathless at his wisdom.

115

He kept nothing from her. She held back nothing. She asked no question he could not or would not answer. Time after time, she watched as he went to worship the Lord God before the altar, and every day her questions grew more profound as the very wisdom of God poured from Solomon's magnificent mind into hers.

When at last she was ready to return to her own land, she experienced a sinking feeling of inadequacy for the first time in her successful life. The Queen had brought rich gifts to Solomon — great stores of spices and precious stones and gold in the equivalent of three and a half million dollars. But as she stood before him to say good-by, her offering seemed pitifully small — she had received so much from him. Not only in new material wealth, but in wisdom, in knowledge.

"I feel I have brought you nothing but my hungry heart, Sire," she said as they parted.

Sheba did bring her hungry heart, and although we know only that she went back to her own country, I choose to believe her hunger was met.

* * * * * * * * *

There are as many shades of opinion as to the untold portion of the story of the Arabian queen as there are versions of her encounter with Solomon. Some writers contend rather strongly that she did *not* come to know the Lord God who had granted such wisdom to the king of Israel. Others intimate that she took back to her own land the knowledge of His name, but no change in her own life. We are told in the Scriptures that she cried: "Blessed be the Lord your God, who has delighted in you and set you on the throne of Israel! Because the Lord loved Israel forever, he has made you king, that you may execute justice and righteousness." These apparently were her parting words to Solomon, right after she gave him the gold and spices and precious stones.

116

Many contend that Sheba herself did not encounter the living God during her visit to Israel, but rather that she merely "acknowledged" God. Well, that's all right, but what can we lose by allowing our own knowledge of the limitless love of God in Jesus Christ to light up this ancient story? Undoubtedly, Sheba took home with her a mind filled with the very wisdom of God. Solomon had prayed for wisdom, and his prayer had been answered. There was no possible way Sheba could have departed without the wisdom of the Lord God of Israel in her own hungry heart. Can we separate God from His wisdom?

Now, certainly I have no intention of wading into a sticky theological discussion, but think this through: Sheba, herself, said, "Because the Lord loved Israel . . ."

". . . the Lord *loved* . . ."

How many Old Testament people had caught onto the fact that God *loved?* They were aware of His power; they believed that He punished. But love? Love broke over the human race when Jesus came to earth to demonstrate the fact that through all the years when men worshiped Him as a God of vengeance, He *had been* a God of love. There should be no confusion now, but there was every reason for confusion in Sheba's time. The Lord God was still the "haunter of the Jew's black mountain tops." He dwelt for the Israelites in burning bushes and pillars of fire. The concept of God's universal love had not been released across the earth to the common man, and yet the Queen of Sheba knew that God loved. Could she have gone home without something of the nature of the living God in her heart if she knew that?

No one knows for sure, but it is somehow vital to me to believe that she received from Solomon, in those twilight years before Christ, a touch of God's own life. You are free to believe what you like, but didn't the wise men come from her land to seek the Child Jesus?

Either way, one thing seems clear for us today from

117

the story of the Queen of Sheba. A woman with an open, hungry heart and an open, receptive mind *will* have access to the wisdom of God. Perhaps I should have said *does* have access to the very wisdom of God. Wisdom, as I understand it, isn't necessarily being clever or smart or brilliant. To have true wisdom is to know how to *act*. To know how to *be*.

Another word for us which I consider very important is that nothing whatever is to be gained by doubting the spiritual depth of another person. Can we possibly know *how* God saves? Can we possibly know His mind or His methods? I've been a follower of Jesus Christ for twenty years, and I still shudder and grow uneasy when I hear someone "decide" about another's spiritual state. It's a risky business, a great waste, and it belittles the God of love whose desire is to invade every human heart.

Jesus, as you know, had quite a bit to say about this. He even went so far as to say that this "Queen of the South" would be qualified to sit in judgment upon the generation of dullards to which Jesus poured out His energies. At least, Sheba made an enormous effort to discover God. Would the God you follow push her aside?

Huldah

...discerning reality

Huldah

...discerning reality

From her house in the Second Quarter, the residental section of Jerusalem in front of the Temple, Huldah, the wife of Shallum, could hear the sounds ringing from inside the high-vaulted Temple walls. She could smell the tangy, freshly planed cedar, and in the courtyard Huldah watched the pile of ripped-out, rotted boards grow day by day. King Josiah, whose wardrobe her husband kept, was repairing the house of God.

"Such work on the Temple is long overdue," Huldah spoke to Shallum as they shared their noon meal.

"Indeed it is," her husband said, breaking off a second piece of fresh baked bread. "King Josiah has done well. I could have told you two years ago when, as a mere lad, he set about cleaning out the corruption in his own court that the young ruler would not stop until he had tried to bring our people back together in the Lord God."

Huldah nodded emphatically. "King Josiah is a man of God — not like his predecessor, King Manasseh. Our Temple was a disgrace before the Lord when the young king began his reign. Look out there at the waste they're hauling away — a disgrace before the Lord God!"

As Huldah and Shallum sat watching, five men in royal

121

clothing, one of them clutching a roll of old parchment, hurried across the courtyard of the Temple and straight to Huldah's door.

Shallum stood up. "It's Hilkiah, the high priest, and four men with him."

"I wonder what they want of us?" Huldah asked.

When the men had been seated and offered food, Hilkiah told them the story. The crumbling scrolls which he refused to put down had been found, he said, by the workmen repairing the Temple. The king had sent him and the four messengers to consult with Huldah. "The king wants you to verify that these are indeed the book of the law given to our fathers through Moses. As soon as it was found, the faithful workmen rushed it to Shaphan here, the temple secretary, who took it to the king."

Hilkiah held the parchments out to Huldah.

"But why did the king choose me, a woman?" she asked.

"Why not?" her husband asked. "You are a prophetess of God as well as a teacher and counselor, Huldah."

"Shallum is right," the high priest said. "And the king has selected you. You have no choice but to examine the book. More than that, you are to interpret it. What it says is fearful for both Israel and Judah. The king will not rest until you prophesy. He rent his clothes when Shaphan read from what is written here. King Josiah has done all he knows to do to unite Judah and Israel — to force the people to give up their idol worship and return to worship the Lord our God together."

"I know some of what he has done," young Ahikam, Shaphan's son, spoke up. "I went with King Josiah on his journey around the land, and with my own eyes I saw him smash idols, grind them into dust, and sprinkle the dust over the graves of those who had worshiped before them. He is a man of God, but because he fears God, he trembles for himself and all his people now that my father has read from these scrolls!"

122

"Please read and tell us what it means, Prophetess," Asaiah, the king's servant, pleaded. "My lord, the king, is so troubled."

"We are all troubled, ma'am," Achbor, the son of Micaiah, pleaded with his dark eyes. "What is written there has filled us all with fear."

As the men jabbered, Huldah had been reading the scrolls, and as she went on reading in silence, one after another of the five messengers fell silent and watched her intently.

Finally she stood and began to speak: "Thus says the Lord, the God of Israel: 'Tell the man who sent you to me, Thus says the Lord, Behold, I will bring evil upon this place and upon its inhabitants, all the words of the book which the king of Judah has read. Because they have forsaken me and have burned incense to other gods, that they might provoke me to anger with all the work of their hands, therefore my wrath will be kindled against this place, and it will not be quenched.' "

The men stared at one another and at Huldah. She had verified the authenticity of the book of the law! "Thus says the Lord," she had repeated twice. It was God's word to them.

Huldah looked at her husband, Shallum, at Hilkiah, the high priest, then at Shaphan and his son, at Achbor, and last of all at Asaiah, the king's own body servant. For a long moment, no one spoke. Then Huldah, rerolling the scroll, said in a strong, authoritative voice: " 'But as to the king of Judah, who sent you to inquire of the Lord, thus shall you say to him, Thus says the Lord, the God of Israel: Regarding the words which you have heard, because your heart was penitent, and you humbled yourself before the Lord, when you heard how I spoke against this place, and against its inhabitants . . . and you have rent your clothes and wept before me, I also have heard you, says the Lord.' "

123

"But what does that mean, Huldah?" Hilkiah demanded.

" 'Thus says the Lord,' " Huldah repeated, " 'behold, I will gather you to your fathers, and you shall be gathered to your grave in peace, and your eyes shall not see all the evil which I will bring upon this place.' "

"Does that mean my lord, the king, will die soon?" Asaiah cried.

"It does not say that," Huldah said quietly. "The Lord God has simply promised our king that because of his own humility and faith nothing terrible shall befall Israel or Judah during his lifetime."

Filled with joy and hope, the five men returned to the king with the encouraging news.

Backed up by the reassuring words of Huldah, the Lord's prophetess, devout King Josiah carried out the most thorough reformation of worship that Judah had ever known. The woman, Huldah, had given him the word of God on which to build his reformation, and the young king went resolutely ahead.

* * * * * * * * * *

The substance of what Huldah interpreted for King Josiah that day is contained for us in the Book of Deuteronomy. How the scroll got hidden in the Temple, no one really knows. Prophets may have put it there, or another good king of Israel, Hezekiah, may have had his reformers reduce principles of the law to writing and conceal it in the Temple for safekeeping.

None of this is particularly relevant, to what God may be saying to women today through His prophetess Huldah. It is irrelevant in this book for us to discuss the possible meaning of the dire threat to Israel and Judah because of their years of idol worship. We are concerned with Huldah, the woman. Actually, very little is known about her except that her husband, Shallum, took care of the king's wardrobe (no small job in those days), and that she possibly (according to Jewish tradition) was a teacher, or

124

perhaps a counselor of women. She is said to have sat in
public places waiting for troubled Hebrew women to come
to her to learn about the Lord God. Of course, she was
also a true prophetess.

One thing is certain: Huldah was no ordinary woman
wrapped up in her own concerns and problems. She was
a woman of God. She lived close to His heart, her own
heart open and listening for what He might have to say
to her, or through her for someone else, as in the case
of King Josiah. Huldah could not have been trapped and
preoccupied with her own troubles, or she would never
have sat on a street corner waiting for other women to
spill their difficulties out to her. She had troubles, I'm sure.
Anyone who listens hour after hour to the woes of others
has problems! Her husband, Shallum, was not a rich man.
His position with the king was menial. She must have
done her own work, and housework in those days did not
do itself as now. Huldah had to have problems, but she
lived above them, not under them. And her discernment
was so clear, so sharp, and so accurate that the king went
to her first and not to any of the numerous male prophets
available to him.

King Josiah's father was an idol worshiper named Amon,
who was murdered by his own servants because of it.
This could have caused the young king to doubt the wisdom of men — even prophets — to lean toward taking
counsel from a respected woman. Surely the tragic end
of his father's life caused him to turn toward the Lord
God and away from idols. Perhaps his mother, Jedidah,
was a devout woman, which could have made him think
of Huldah first. All these influences may have contributed,
but much more plausible to me is the probability that he
called Huldah over anyone else because he knew her. 125
Knew her to be a first-hander with the Lord God, un-
cluttered by typical woman concerns, filled with integrity
and wisdom. I like to think Huldah was something like

my beloved friend, Dr. Anna Mow, who, with all her wisdom and intellect and learning, keeps a livable home and loves to cook big, delicious meals, to can and freeze food as much as she enjoys writing books that give us words and thoughts and ideas straight from the heart of the Father.

God's word for us through Huldah is that He can get through to women like her. She keeps an orderly *inner* house. When God needed to speak to King Josiah through Huldah, there was no clutter to get in His way.

Huldah, like my friend Anna, did not even clutter God's wisdom with her own. Before every new thought, she made sure she said, "Thus says the Lord." Women like Huldah give God room to act. Their discernments are real — they are free to discern the reality of both God and people. Huldah knew God and she also knew the king — knew it was safe to give him the encouragement he needed to pursue his high course of reuniting his people around the God of their fathers.

It is impossible to discern reality in God and to come up with fuzzy notions about people. True discernment encompasses all reality.

Women of the New Testament

Anna

...the creative widow

Anna

...the creative widow

Bracing herself with one arm against the marble column of Solomon's porch on the eastern side of the Temple in Jerusalem, the aging prophetess, Anna, turned to greet her elderly friend, Simeon, who was slowly climbing the steps from the street. Anna did not walk toward him, and Simeon did not hurry. Neither of them had ever hurried through the years of their lives. Too much of eternity had invaded their days for haste. They geared their comings and goings to the Lord God, depending, as children depend, upon His guidance — so abandoned to the divine will, so sensitive to the divine whisper that each lived hourly within the quiet order of holy rhythm.

Slowly, Simeon shuffled toward his devout friend, a smile crinkling the thin skin around his faded eyes. "Shalom, Anna," he said as he stopped to chat with her in the comfortable way they had spoken together for the more than fifty years in which they had seen each other daily in the Temple. "There will be a fine sunset for us to enjoy — just enough clouds to make the light glow."

"Yes, Simeon. Clouds are needed in order to make a

129

sunset beautiful. Thanks be to the Lord our God for clouds, I say."

Simeon chuckled. "You've earned the right to say that, Anna. You've allowed the Lord God to make your life beautiful — and heaven knows it's been full of clouds."

"Some of them very dark clouds, Simeon," the old woman answered, not sorrowfully but with a smile.

"The kind of darkness only one widowed so young could know," Simeon said, looking at the sky. "I have known you all these years, though, my friend, and not once have I known you to complain of your widowhood."

She sighed. "There has been nothing about which to fuss, old man. I had seven years of happiness with my husband and all the other years between his death and my eighty-fourth birthday last week to enjoy the Lord God."

"You've been in the Temple most of the day, I suppose," Simeon said, pulling his cloak around his thin throat against the chill evening breeze that had begun to scatter leaves along the paved floor of Solomon's porch.

"All day," she replied. "And all day my joy has grown. Oh, Simeon, old man — the Messiah comes soon! The Spirit of our God has assured me now, even as He has assured you, that I, too, will not die until I have seen Him." Her thin, veined hands were clasped and her face glowed.

"We are old enough, both of us, Anna, for the people to call us childish for our faith in the swift coming of the Messiah, but it is not we who are loose in the head — it is they. He comes, *very* soon now, He comes. I grow weaker daily. My time to leave draws closer. And as it does, so does the coming of our Messiah. God has promised I will not die until I have seen Him, and I am going soon."

130

Anna turned to look at her friend. "It is all joy, Simeon, going or staying because of the Lord our God."

Day after day, the old friends met somewhere in the Temple to speak of the coming of the promised Messiah. To speak with mounting joy of it, with heightened anticipation, with deepening confidence that it would be soon. And on one certain day, as Anna prayed in the Court of the Women, the partitioned east portion of the inner court where both men and women could pray, she felt a gentle hand on her shoulder and turned to see her friend, Simeon, standing beside her.

"My old heart pounds this day, Anna," he whispered. "Could this be the day He will come? Do you have any word from the Lord God for me, my friend?"

Anna smiled. "Only the same assurance that it will be soon, Simeon."

"Then I will go to my own prayers and let you return to yours."

Anna watched him hobble away and tried to go back to her prayers, but her mind would not focus. A great excitement seemed to grip her so that her bent old body shook. Suddenly she turned to look in the direction of the wide stair that led from the Court of the Women to the Court of the Gentiles, fully expecting to see a heavenly sign. All she saw was a simple Hebrew couple crossing the lower court, slowly, almost shyly, as though awed by the size and splendor of the Temple. In her arms, the young mother carried her baby. They have come for the purification, Anna thought, and was glad in her heart that one more man child would be the Lord's own. Anna had borne no children, and through the years, some of her happiest experiences had been to watch the young couples bring their sons to be dedicated to the Lord God.

She watched this humble, plainly dressed man and woman as they started up the stair to the Court of the Women, and then from the other side of the high partition she saw Simeon staring at the same two parents with their babe.

131

Anna watched Simeon cross the upper court and hurry dangerously close to the top of the stair as though he had expected this very man and woman at this very moment. He's going to fall! Anna caught her breath as Simeon lost his balance, then relaxed when the father of the child put his strong arm around Simeon to steady him. Unmindful of his narrow escape, Simeon raised both hands in the air and began to praise God in a loud voice, and Anna found herself hurrying toward the little group of people at the top of the stair — hurrying, with almost no pain in her stiff old legs.

When she reached them, the young mother was smiling as though for a deeper reason than that she held a new son in her arms, and Simeon was crying out: "Lord, now lettest thou thy servant depart in peace, according to thy word; for mine eyes have seen thy salvation which thou hast prepared in the presence of all peoples!"

Anna gasped as she saw her friend reach for the child, take him in his arms, and lift his radiant old face to God.

"For mine eyes have *seen* thy salvation . . . a light for revelation to the Gentiles, and for glory to thy people Israel!"

The young mother stood wide-eyed, marveling at what Simeon had said of her son.

"He knows, Mary!" her kind faced husband said. "This old man is a man of God; he knows the child is no ordinary child."

Anna stood transfixed, her eyes drinking in the beauty of the baby's face, as Simeon gently handed the child back to his mother, saying: "Behold, this child is set for the fall and rising of many in Israel, and for a sign that is spoken against — " And he stopped speaking and looked deeply into the young mother's eyes. ". . . and a sword will pierce through your own soul also, that thoughts out of many hearts may be revealed."

Anna saw the young woman frown slightly and look

132

for some explanation from her husband. There was none. For a long moment, no one spoke, and then Anna, as though the very joy of heaven had been released within her, turned and hurried down the stair, across the Court of the Gentiles, and onto the porch, giving thanks to God and telling everyone she saw that the redemption of Israel had come to live among them!

* * * * * * * * * * *

The very first person to tell the Good News of the coming of Jesus Christ was a woman. I make note of this not to give us cause for feeling spiritually superior — the very first person to obey the serpent in the Garden was a woman too, don't forget. The important aspect of Anna's life for us today is, in my opinion, the *quality* of her life.

If you will read almost any old or new commentary on Anna the prophetess, you will find words of praise for her spirituality, her dedication to the Lord God, her daily prayer and fasting. All admirable, of course, and evidently true, but these things do not impress me as being the most important characteristics of this important woman. Her deep spirituality, her prayer life, and her devotion to God are *fruits* of what Anna was really like inside, as a human being. I have long felt that we only increase our own guilt when we attempt to flail ourselves for not being as "holy" as someone else whose pious virtues are extolled before us as a challenge to deepen our own commitment to God. When we say (however "spiritual" we try to make it sound), "Oh, I know I should do more for God," or, "I need to pray more," are we being realistic or are we merely trying to add on from the outside?

I don't think the remarkable thing about Anna is her regular attendance in the Temple, her fasting, her constant prayer. To me, the remarkable thing about her which can be of help to us today is that Anna just wouldn't have made it at all without this steady communion with

133

God! Those of us who have faced tragedy of any kind — particularly those of you who are widows — *know* that nothing heals the wounds like being consciously with God. Anna prayed and stayed close to the Temple because she had to. I'm sure she would be the first to laugh at extolling as virtue what to her was sheer necessity.

Still, I am equally as certain that Anna, the prophetess, had shining virtue and, to me, it shows in her *willingness* not to be a tragedy herself. She was married only seven short years when her husband died. It would have been quite understandable if she had either looked for another husband or had sunk into self-pity over her desolate state. She did neither. Not that there is anything wrong with a second marriage. This is scarcely the point here. Apparently Anna didn't even consider it. But neither did she give in to self-concern so that she became a tragedy herself. Tragedy comes to everyone sooner or later, but the spirit oriented in God need not become a tragedy, need not make life wretched for those nearby, need not waste the remaining years.

Anna used her tragedy creatively. Used it? Yes. She permitted her heartbreak to force her to God — not as a husband substitute, but as her Friend and Comforter and Lord. There is a subtle difference here. I have known widows who *try* to "make God my husband." This is not only unhealthy, it is impossible, and it demeans God. God is never a substitute. He is God. He does not act like a husband; He acts like God. And the reason I am sure Anna used the tragedy of her widowhood creatively, the reason I am sure she made no belittling effort to put God in the role of a substitute for her dead husband, is that her life did not turn inward — it turned outward. Now, I admit some writers insist that Luke's brief description of Anna indicates that she lived a totally mystical, aesthetic, shut-away life of prayer and devotion. I couldn't disagree more. And the reason I disagree, the reason I

134

am convinced that Anna lived creatively toward others, not shut **away** from life, has nothing to do with what Luke said — except as he tells us what Anna *did*. The minute she saw the Messiah, the Baby Jesus, she ran right out where the people were to spread the Good News to *them*. She didn't cloister herself to "enjoy her spiritual experience" alone; she hurried to the people.

One of the sorrows of young widows, I understand, is that they cannot bear children — cannot be creative. Anna disproves this to me. Real creativity always reaches outward to bless, never inward to please.

Anna was a widow at an early age, but I see her as one of the most creative women in the whole of human history.

the Widow of Nain

...some thoughts on death

the Widow of Nain

...some thoughts on death

Its flat-topped houses and shops built mostly of field-stone, the Galilean village of Nain spread across a portion of the northwest slope of the Hill of Moreh, known as Little Hermon. There were no walls around Nain, and its people lived their routine daily lives in full view of one of the most breath-taking scenes in all Galilee. One could look for miles across the wide plains to the northwest toward Mt. Carmel, to the north toward the hills behind Nazareth just six miles distant, to the northeast past Mt. Tabor all the way to the snowy heights of Mt. Hermon, and south to Mt. Gilboa.

At any hour of the day, the people of Nain could "lift up their eyes unto the hills." Even when clouds obscured them, the hills and mountains were still there, like protective arms around the men, women, and children who drove their donkeys and pushed their fruit and vegetable carts through the twisting, hard-packed streets of the village of Nain. And when the sun began to drop behind the dark slopes of Mt. Carmel and the Nazareth hills, shadows fell quickly. Too quickly on this evening in early spring, as a small funeral procession wound its way

139

through the gate of the tiny city and out onto the road that leads east to the old burying ground.

The first anguished explosion of sorrow for the woman who trudged close behind the hand-carried bier was over. She and her neighbors had wailed and wept together, clenching their fists in the agony of disbelief that the widow's son had died. Nothing they did for him had helped. The dread disease had gripped him, and neither their ministering nor his strong, young body could hold it off. The boy was dead — lying stiff and straight on the open bier, wrapped in burial clothes, a napkin over his face. He was all his mother had for support, for companionship, for joy. And so she had wept until they feared she, too, would become ill, and her friends had wept and screamed their grief at the heavens all through that first black night.

Now, her head draped in a mourning cloth, the heartbroken mother walked silently beside the slowly moving bier. She did not weep. She was too tense, too afraid, too full of dread at the moment just ahead — the worst moment of all — when she would have to see her beloved son's body buried out of her sight forever. She walked stiffly; her hands clenched together until her knuckles were white. Trying not to think, walking, walking toward the inevitable moment when for the last time she would somehow have to find strength to turn away from the grave and go home without him. Her upper garment hung torn from her shoulders as, according to custom, she had rent it while the last sad offices were done. Lovingly, she had helped her friends stretch the still warm body on the ground, had insisted upon holding his dear hands as the nails were cut, had stood by while his body was washed, anointed, and wrapped in the best cloth she could buy. She had sat on the floor, eating no meat, drinking not one sip of wine. The scant meal she had eaten had to be without prayer and as far from the boy's dead body

140

as possible. Once she had gone to her neighbor's house to eat. Today, she was too exhausted, and so she had done her best by the custom — the one piece of bread was eaten with her back turned to the corpse. She could afford only one mourning woman and two flutes, and to the minor motif of the piped lamentations, the hired mourner chanted: "Alas, the lion! Alas, the hero!"

Her son had been her lion, her hero — her life. And now he was gone. Back in her empty house, the chairs and couches had been reversed, turned upside down. The minutes were moving by; they moved nearer the cemetery; in no time at all now, she would have to return to that empty house alone. It could not be her son lying motionless on the myrtle-draped wicker bier being carried so tenderly now by their shoeless neighbors toward the burying ground. Almost any minute now, she would have to accept the fact that he was gone — the merry laughter silenced, the quick hands cold and still on his quiet breast. The flutes seemed louder; the shouted chants of the mourner made her head ache, but somehow she kept walking at the head of the bier, taking her boy to his grave. The tears began to flow again, and her weeping shook her frail shoulders, drew on her strength.

The sun was only a great red ball now, slipping behind the hills. They must hurry while there was still light.

Suddenly the neighbor walking beside her stopped and grabbed the widow's arm. "What is it?" she asked. "Why have we stopped walking?"

"Look!" the neighbor whispered. "Look at the Rabbi coming toward you. He has stopped the procession and is coming this way!"

From the direction of Endor on the road from Capernaum, a small band of men and their Teacher, followed by an enormous crowd of people, had reached the outskirts of Nain and stopped at the sight of the sad little parade of mourners. The Rabbi spoke for a moment to

141

one of His men, and was now striding deliberately toward the widow.

"Do not weep, woman," He called before He reached her side. "Do not weep any more!"

His voice was so full of gentleness, authority, and compassion, that the widow could only stare at Him, her swollen eyes wide and bewildered.

Without another word to her, He walked directly up to the bier and, in defiance of the Jewish rabbis' fear of contamination, laid His hand on it and said, "Young man, I say to thee, arise!"

Before her eyes, the widow's son sat up on the bier, ripped aside his grave clothes, and began to talk to her. The Stranger helped her son down from the bier with His own hands and led him to his mother.

And the mourners forgot their mourning as they began to glorify God, shouting: "A great prophet has risen among us! God has visited his people!"

＊ ＊ ＊ ＊ ＊ ＊ ＊ ＊ ＊ ＊

Much has been written about the confrontation that evening on the road to Nain between the Spirit of Life and the spirit of death. Death could not survive in His presence!

It is true, the widow's son was the first recorded resurrection performed by Jesus, and, as a result of it, the throng which had followed the Master after the remarkable healing of the centurion's servant in Capernaum had their faith strengthened at Nain. Undoubtedly, many of those friends and neighbors who carried the bier and walked beside the widow began to believe at the moment Jesus gave back her son. All these truths are relevant and evident.

142 But I have known of women who, in their own grief and agony following the death of a loved one, refuse even to think of the widow's joy. It infuriates them! It makes them envious and confused. They feel frustrated,

"put upon" by God. Why would He do this for one woman and not for them? Why must their own faith seem
to go unrewarded when this widow, who didn't even
know who Jesus was, got her son back alive and healthy?

"I don't dare think about that story," one bitter young
mother said to me once. "If I do, I begin to hate God
for playing favorites! If He did that once so long ago,
why does He refuse to do it now?"

Only last week I had a letter from a young widow
whose husband was killed in Viet Nam through an error
in orders — killed by his own men. "He was a genuine
Christian, and his mother and I prayed constantly for
his safety. Why does God play favorites by saving some
men who couldn't care less about Christianity and letting
my husband be killed?"

I had already received several letters from another girl
named Julie, whose fiancé, Don, also an authentic Christian, had been killed by the same kind of freak accident
in the same war. "My whole life is torn in two," Julie
wrote, "but I can't question God because Don was His
child."

Does God play favorites?

The question is as understandable as it is groundless.
No. God plays no favorites. And although — in all the
years men have been exploring the question of God's protection — no one has answered it, I think we can get this
much from the story of the Widow of Nain and Jesus:
God *does* work in the haphazard. I have written that line
before, and some people have been freed by it; others
have been angered. But what is needed I feel, is for us
to recognize what the *haphazard* might really be. If we
are careless, fuzzy in our thinking, the word *haphazard*
means life with no plan, no pattern, no guiding intelligence behind it. Well, much of life does look that way.
You see, Julie and Don believed (and had every reason
to believe) that God had brought them together. They

143

were to have been married when Don came home, and if Don had not been killed, I have no doubt whatever but that God would have blessed their marriage. Don did not come home, though. He was killed because some American buddy missed an order. Well, where was God? Just where He has always been — with us. With Don at the instant of his death, and with Julie when she learned of it.

I have no pat answers anymore about anything. Perhaps, hopefully, that is the beginning of true intelligence. But the more I discover about the real nature of God, the more I realize that more *reverence* is required of us — a greater sense of the holiness of God. Not holiness in the area of His purity only, but in the area of God's intelligence and actions. Our God is a whole God with a whole plan for a whole world. Could it be that what *appears* to be haphazard to us is whole to God? After all, we can't see as God sees. We can't know as God knows. He has told us that His ways are higher than our ways, His thoughts higher than our thoughts.

I have no specific answer to those anguished cries accusing God of favoritism, but I do see this much: We dare not try to understand God's doing this or not doing that. It is not that our daring to question God makes Him angry. This is pathetically immature thinking. To fear God's anger when our hearts cry out with legitimate questions is to demonstrate our total lack of knowledge of what He is really like. I say we *dare* not question His actions simply because we would not understand the answer if we got it in letters fifty feet high!

There is only one way to understand events that tear our lives apart; surely, there is only one way to be able to accept these events without selfpity. Julie made it. very clear: "I cannot question God because Don was His child."

Now, of course, I don't know all she meant when she

wrote that short sentence. I know what it means to me. It does *not* mean that Don was a super-Christian. It means the boy belonged to the Father who had His mind on him every minute. To me, what Julie was saying was that Don did not belong to an easily irritated judge; he belonged to the Father. If you have read any of my other books, you know I do not believe God punishes by grief or sorrow or pain. He is a God of love, and His only punishment is by the "cords of love." Just because we cannot always understand the *events* that bring us sorrow seems a slim reason for doubting that God is still love and still in charge. There is nothing in the New Testament (and this is God's latest word to us) which indicates that a "good" Christian is going to be spared anything or that an evil man or woman will be punished. Jesus came to show us a higher way, and *love covers*.

Joanna

...the woman who returned her gift

Luke 8:1 - 3; 23:55; 24:10; Matthew 14:1, 2

Joanna

...the woman who returned her gift

Joanna, in a flowing, blue dress, caught at her waist
by a wide, bright girdle, walked first to the window of the
dining room, then back to the table spread for dinner.
The food had already been served. If her husband, Chuza,
didn't get there soon, the lamb would be cold. She moved
the large bowl of mulberries and melon chunks to a spot
more to her liking and set two pitchers of honey and the
leban beside it. She would serve Chuza no more date or
nut candy for a while. He had thickened a bit in his
waistline lately.

At last, she heard his heavy, quick footsteps in the hall-
way, and then he was beside her. After an absent-minded
kiss on her forehead, her husband began to eat and talk
too fast.

"I know I'm late, Joanna, and if there were another
position as fruitful as being King Herod's steward anywhere in all the land, I can assure you I'd leave him
tomorrow!"

Joanna studied Chuza's broad, kind face for a long moment. "What is it now, my dear? Did he keep you again
while he tried — and failed again — to understand your
accounts?"

149

Chuza broke off a huge piece of fresh bread and stuffed it in his mouth. "No, no, no. Nothing so simple as that. I simply needed his signature on a document, and I was absolutely unable to get the man to concentrate!"

"Too much wine again?"

"The normal amount. Too much, yes. But the king has a crazy idea in his tortured head, and no one can get him to forget it. I think he could lose his senses, Joanna. I really do. Can you guess what's tormenting him now?"

"Don't you think you should finish your meal first, Chuza? I do hate to see you bolt your food when you're so upset."

"Never mind my food. Can you guess what King Herod announced to us today?"

"No, my dear. I've stopped trying."

"He called all of us who work with him — even the menial servants — and informed us that your Master, Jesus of Nazareth, is really John the Baptist risen from the dead!"

Joanna stopped eating. "Why would the king think a thing like that?"

"Because of all the miracles the Rabbi has done. Even you who follow Him must know people are talking everywhere. A Teacher cannot go about the country healing the sick, causing the blind to see, unstopping deaf ears, straightening crippled legs — " Chuza laid his hand on Joanna's arm tenderly. "I meant no harm by what I said. I, of all people, am grateful that your Master straightened your crippled body, my dear. But He is not healing King Herod. The king is growing more peculiar every day!"

"This is not my Master's fault, Chuza. After all, King Herod had that good man, John the Baptist, murdered. I don't wonder that his poor mind is haunted."

150

"Perhaps so, Joanna, but I do wish the Rabbi would move to another part of the country — away from Jerusalem — and give the king some peace. I'd be a bit more peaceful too, just because the king might get his mind on someone else for a while."

"The Master is leaving soon, Chuza, and I am going with Him."

Her husband jumped to his feet. "You are going with Him? You must be losing your senses too, Joanna!"

"No, I've never been saner in all my life. After what He has done for me, how can I *not* go with Him on His journeys to heal and teach other people as ill and as much in darkness as I was?" She stood up. "There is no point in trying to change my mind, my husband. I am going with the Master, to care for Him as I am able. Susanna is going too. And a woman named Mary, whose devil-possessed mind He healed one day in Magdala. There will be others along the way. He needs me, and I am going with Him wherever He goes."

Up and down the dusty countryside, throughout Judea and Galilee, Joanna and the other women traveled with Jesus and His disciples. Some of them, like Joanna, were women of means and could assist His work financially; others, like Mary Magdalene, had only their energies to give. They all did what they could, stopping by creeks and rivers to wash clothes, mending garments by firelight at night when the party stopped to rest. Often, the women hurried on ahead to make arrangements for a night's lodging or a meeting place in the next town or village.

They were with Him when Mary and Martha sent for Jesus to come to the bedside of their dying brother, Lazarus. They stood at the edge of the crowd around the tomb when He cried, "Lazarus, come out!" They were with the Master on His last trip before the Passover, and Joanna and Susanna assisted Peter and John in planning with Mary of Jerusalem for the Lord and the disciples to eat their Last Supper together in Mary's second floor dining room.

151

Joanna and the other women let Him out of their sight only when He was dragged before Pilate. They were there, at the foot of His cross, watching Him die without one move to defend Himself. When Joseph of Arimathaea had the beloved, limp body laid in his own grave in the garden, Joanna and the women stood by weeping and watching.

And when ". . . it was the day of Preparation, and the sabbath was beginning, the women who had come with him from Galilee followed, and saw the tomb, and how his body was laid; then they returned, and prepared spices and ointments. On the sabbath they rested according to the commandment. But on the first day of the week, at early dawn, they went to the tomb, taking the spices which they had prepared."

Joanna was there with the "other women." She saw the great stone rolled away — the tomb empty. With her own ears she heard the heavenly voices ask: "Why do you seek the living among the dead?"

With her friends, Joanna ran to tell His disciples that their Master was risen as He said.

"Peter, John, don't you remember?" she asked when it was obvious the men did not believe what the women had seen. "Doesn't even one of you men remember what He told us over and over again on the way? Why, while we were still in Galilee together, the Master told us that the Son of Man must be delivered into the hands of sinful men and be crucified. He told us this; don't you remember at all? He said He would be crucified, but that on the third day He would rise again. He is risen! The Lord is risen!"

152   Mary Magdalene was there when Joanna pleaded with the disciples to take their word for it   Mary Magdalene believed. The men did not. Susanna believed. The men did not.

Joanna and her friends had done what they could for Him, and they believed.

* * * * * * * * * *

Could God's word for us today from these brief Scriptural mentions of Joanna and her friends be the key to believing faith? And could this key to believing faith have to do with exchanged gifts? With exchanged lives?

We do not know the nature of Joanna's affliction. She could have been crippled, desperately ill, blind, deaf, or — as I believe Mary of Magdala to have been — mentally ill. Whatever caused her suffering, she had exchanged her tormented life for the whole, free, healthy life of Christ. This may seem a bad exchange, to have received so much for so little, but when His touch falls on a human spirit, even the "little" can become great. The blind *do* see. The deaf ears *are* unstopped. The once crippled bodies *do* stand erect. The sick minds *can* think again.

Could it be that faith in the risen Christ was easier for these women because they had needed so much from Him? I believe it was. True, they saw the empty tomb with their own eyes, and the disciples had only a woman's word for it, but the woman could have believed the lie that His body had been stolen. They chose to believe the word of God rather than the word of man, and I am sure they found it easier to do because they had received so much from Jesus.

So, then, is receiving the secret of faith? As with the forgiven harlot, did these women love more because their needs had been greater than the needs of the disciples who followed Jesus? Yes, but there is more. These women — not by searching or asking professional counselors for answers, but by acting on the one motivation of love — 153 happened upon the whole secret of a believing faith. They received fully, but in turn, they gave fully. Women were not educated in those days. Joanna and Susanna and Mary of Magdala and the other women did not do what they did for Jesus because they were practicing a technique for faith-building which they had studied in some profound treatise. They had received no professional counsel, had written no letters asking advice. They did what their hearts directed them to do — what any woman can do; they loved, and loving, they gave to Him in return.

They did what they could do. They did the only thing they could do — exchange their gifts.

Could it be that the men who followed Jesus, even though they were His chosen ones, were attempting only to follow Him intellectually? This in no way discredits them. And I feel there is ample evidence in the Scriptures that this could have been the case. After all, didn't they badger Him with questions the enlightened heart would have known already? Pentecost took care of the unenlightened hearts of the disciples. Undoubtedly, the coming of the Holy Spirit into the very lives of the women lighted their hearts still more. But in this instance, I believe these faithful women unknowingly had stumbled onto the secret of a sturdy faith.

They received, but they also gave in return. There is a shining secret in exchanged lives when one Life is the very Life of God Himself.

the Samaritan woman

...moment of recognition

the Samaritan woman
...moment of recognition

Carefully, she eased open the sagging door of her mud cottage and looked up and down the narrow side street. If she met a man on her way to the well to draw water, it wouldn't matter. No man had ever snubbed her! But she did not want to meet a woman. Even the peasant women of the village of Sychar, poor like herself, would turn their eyes away when she passed. If they were in a group, on sight of her, they would begin to buzz, and she needed no one to tell her what they were saying.

The street was empty, and so the once beautiful town harlot, her water jar balanced easily on her dark head, moved quickly down the narrow lane toward Jacob's well, a half mile or so from the village. Her worn sandals slapped against the hot stones of the street as she walked, not as gracefully as she had once walked, but defiantly to cover the shame she still felt because of her faded beauty, her dirty, unkempt clothing — the decadence of her life.

"So, my hair straggles and my headdress is stained," she spoke aloud into the hot, silent afternoon. "I still have coins on it!" The woman tossed her head so that the coins jangled. "And I have a new sash — " Her laugh was hard, defensive. "Too bright and gaudy *they'd* say, but what do I care?"

157

She hummed a silly tune all the way to the well, oblivious of the beautiful countryside and the olive green valley of Shechem stretching in the shadows below her own Samaritan holy mountain, Gerizim, and the hated Jews' holy mountain, Moriah.

A few feet from the steps that led down to the ancient well, she stopped singing and inspected the figure sitting on the stone well rim. It's all right, she thought. It's a man. I'll ignore him — unless he speaks to me.

Her jar was almost full of cool water before the Stranger spoke to her. "Give me a drink," He said courteously.

She stared at Him. He was obviously a Jew, but His smile was so kind and He looked so weary and hot, she found it difficult to be insulting — as any Samaritan woman should be to a strange Jew who dared to speak to her. She set down her heavy water pot, planted her hands on her hips, and asked, "How is it that you, a Jew, ask a drink of me, a woman of Samaria?"

Let Him think what He likes, she thought. He can either think I'm surprised *or* angry that He dared speak to me. I don't care.

The Stranger looked at her for a long moment before He replied, "If you knew the gift of God, and who it is that is saying to you, 'Give me a drink,' you would have asked him, and he would have given you living water."

The woman frowned, unable to think what to say next. He went on looking at her, the kind smile still playing around His mouth. She wanted to turn away, to ignore Him, but she felt herself smile a little as she said, "Sir, you have nothing to draw with, and the well is deep; where do you get that living water?" Some of her old cockiness returned. "Are you greater than our father Jacob, who gave us the well, and drank from it himself, and his sons, and his cattle?"

He stopped smiling, and something in His voice was like a tender warning — just for her. "Everyone who

158

drinks of this water," He said, pointing to the well, "will thirst again, but whoever drinks of the water that I shall give him will never thirst."

The woman shifted her position, feeling suddenly like an ungainly girl, and one foot rubbed the dirty instep of the other.

"The water that I shall give him," He went on, "shall become in him a spring of water welling up to eternal life."

She took one eager step toward the Stranger. "Sir, give me this water, that I may not thirst, nor come here to draw — ever again!"

He studied her, but said nothing.

Why doesn't this Jew answer me, she thought anxiously. If He doesn't say something soon, I — I — . "Sir! Sir, *give me this water!*"

At last He spoke, and there was no smile on His face nor in His voice. "Go, call your husband, and come here."

She reeled as though He had struck her, and before she could stop herself, she shrilled: "I have no husband!"

The Stranger smiled again, but in His smile was no trace of mockery, no trace of condemnation, only kindness. It has been so long, she thought, since I've seen *kindness* on anyone's face — toward *me*. I wish He would speak again; oh, I do wish He would speak to me again.

"You are right in saying 'I have no husband,'" He said at last, and she felt as though He had paid her the only sincere compliment of her whole life. "You are right in saying 'I have no husband'; for you have had five husbands, and he whom you now have is not your husband; this you said truly."

The woman sat down abruptly on the wall across the well from where He sat. She breathed as though she had been running; her mouth went dry. *Who was this Stranger?* Who was this hated Jew who could be so kind and so cruel all at once? No! He was not cruel. He must

159

be a prophet! Only a prophet of God could know her as He did, when she had never laid eyes on Him until this very day. Well, she decided, I've had enough of this kind of talk. It's none of His business how many husbands I've had, or whether or not the man I live with now is my husband. I'll change the subject. I'll show Him I can talk on high, philosophical levels too! "Sir," she said as haughtily as she could manage, "I perceive that you are a prophet." When He didn't answer, hoping to start a controversy that had nothing to do with her personally, she said, "*Our* fathers worshiped on this mountain," and she tossed her head toward Gerizim, so that the coins on her headdress jingled. "And *you* say that in Jerusalem is the place where men ought to worship."

He looked toward Mt. Gerizim and then toward Mt. Moriah. I've trapped Him, she thought, and felt pleased with herself. I've got Him on another subject.

He stood up, still looking toward Jerusalem and Mt. Moriah; then He turned slowly around to face her. "Woman," He said, in a voice that made her tremble although it was soft, almost a whisper. "Woman, believe me, the hour is coming when neither on this mountain — " He pointed toward Gerizim, "nor in Jerusalem will you worship the Father."

She frowned. Was He discounting the truth of both the Jews and the Samaritans? Was this a madman?

"You worship what you do not know," He went on. "We worship what we know, for salvation *is* from the Jews."

The woman stiffened.

"But the hour is coming," He went on, "and now is, when the true worshipers will worship the Father in spirit and truth, for such the Father seeks to worship him."

160

Unaccountably, just when she wanted most to run, the hard shell around her heart began to break. If only He would keep on talking to her.

"God is spirit," He said with quiet authority. "And those who worship him must worship in spirit and truth." And then He added: "Not on this mountain or that — in *spirit* and truth."

Suddenly with all her being she wanted what she said next to make this Stranger glad. She could not have explained why, but she wanted Him to be glad over her. Desperately, she longed somehow to please this Man she had never seen before in her life. Her words tumbled out: "Sir, I know that the Messiah is coming — he who is called Christ — and when he comes, he will show us all things!"

He stood before her, His face so open, so vulnerable; she had a wild notion that if she struck Him, His expression would not change. And then He said: "I who speak to you am he."

The blood drained from the woman's face. "You? You — are — the — Christ?"

"I who speak to you am he," the Man repeated.

And before she could find any words to say, a noisy band of men who seemed to be looking for Him came toward them.

"Why are You talking with *her?*" one of the men called.

But she was not insulted this time. It no longer mattered what anyone thought of her. Everything had changed! Everything in all the world had changed. Maybe she too had changed. Forgetting her water pot, she ran as hard as she could back toward Sychar to tell everyone she knew that *she* — the village bad woman — had found the Messiah!

* * * * * * * * * *

What happened when she ran back to her village crying: "Come, see a man who told me all that I ever did!" is well known. The people, on the strength of her rather superficial, but sincere witness to Jesus, came running to find Him too. Even four years later, when the evangelist

161

Philip came to preach in Samaria, the fruits of this woman's witness were still in evidence. I like to think she and Philip knew each other.

But pages have already been written about how her transformed life gave opening to other transformed lives as a result of this one talk she had with Jesus. The word I feel God has for us here is seldom written about, seldom discussed.

Jesus normally waited for a person in need to recognize that need and ask in some degree of faith for its fulfillment. Now, with this woman, He simply did not follow this pattern (no pattern can ever contain Him!).

But I feel we should think for a moment about the possible reason He might have had for pressing His offer upon her. Actually, we could just say that *He knew her* and let it go at that. He knew that although she was a simple, uneducated harlot, she was also a complex human being — as is everyone. Still, He knew the thickness of that shell around her heart. He knew how long she had worked to form it as a protection from further hurt — the kind of hurt that always goes with a life like hers. With any life lived according to one's own rules. He knew also the extreme depth of her need. He knew that if He did not press His offer, she could easily pick up her water pot and saunter away from Him forever.

He knew her.

Now, I feel there are two things here for us:

1. For those who "work" at winning people to Jesus Christ, could it be God is saying: "Don't expect a truly troubled heart to ask for forgiveness in faith at the outset. Don't expect a quick response from someone so damaged by life. Wait. Be patient. Give *Me* time to break through that hard shell. Only I know how!"

2. For those who feel they are too far gone for God to

162

care about them, to want them, to need them, we only have to remember the woman at the well outside Sychar. An immoral woman, middle-aged, unkempt, with dirty hair and a defiant heart — yet the Son of God Himself took great and tender care with her. Not only did He put Himself in the position of asking her for a drink of water, not only did He ignore (as He always did) all the bigoted racial prejudice of His day, not only did He take all the time *she* needed, He pursued her! No one, no one who has ever been born into this earthly life can ever sink too low for the Son of God to seek after. More than all this, so far as I can discover, up until this time in His ministry, Jesus had never before openly declared Himself to be the Christ. He made the all-important admission to the town's most despised woman.

He is not a respecter of persons, but He is always a respecter of hearts.

the Woman with an issue of blood

...the simplicity of faith

Matthew 9:18 - 22; Mark 5:25 - 34; Luke 8:43 - 48

the Woman with an issue of blood

...the simplicity of faith

In a tiny village about seven miles from Capernaum, the light front room of one of the larger houses was filled with women — all busily sewing and, of course, talking.

"Do you remember the pretty young woman who used to walk the seven miles each week to help us with our sewing for the poor and afflicted?" One of the older women posed the question as she deftly cut out a white undergarment. "What was her name — Veronica?"

"Yes," a plump, middle-aged lady answered, biting off a thread. "Poor child! She'd still be coming to help us if she could walk. But do you know she'd been hemorrhaging for all these years?"

"I know all about her trouble," a third woman said. "Her mother is related to my husband's people. She married and had a child when she was twenty. The child died, but the young mother never healed. And for twelve years she and her family have spent every mite they could lay their hands on taking her from one doctor to another."

"And nothing helped at all?"

"Nothing! If anything, the poor little thing grew worse."

"I heard she grew so weak finally, that it was all she could do to walk."

167

"You heard right," their informant declared. "She got so bad it was all she could do to walk."

"Well, is she still living?"

"Yes, the last I heard, but no one expects her to live long. When the blood is depleted, life goes."

"How much money they must have spent on those high-priced astringents!"

"How much indeed, and she has tried them all. All the new medical astringents *and* tonics — all taken as someone addressed her with the words: 'Arise from thy flux!' You know nothing heals without those magic words, but even that did not help poor Veronica."

The middle-aged woman's round face crinkled with pity. "The last I heard — and this was five or six years ago, I suppose — the child was dutifully carrying the ashes of an ostrich egg tied up in a linen rag in summer and in a cotton rag in winter. I don't suppose that did any good either."

"Not a bit. About a year ago, I learned she had given up carrying the ashes. I suppose she has given up everything by now. She could be dead."

For several minutes the ladies sewed in silence, pondering the helplessness of the physicians against the dread diseases that struck down so many of their friends and neighbors.

Then one of them said, "My husband returned from Capernaum yesterday with the news that there is a healer going about the countryside — a Galilean, who by one touch caused the little twelve-year-old daughter of a synagogue ruler named Jairus to rise from the dead!"

"A real healer?" the women gasped. "What's his name?"

168 "My husband didn't catch his name, but it seems this Jairus came to the healer and begged him to come before the child died. I guess he agreed to go — in fact, I believe my husband said the man was on his way to the fine big

house where Jairus lives — but the little girl died before he got there."

The women put down their sewing to listen.

"It seems this teacher or healer or whatever he is was detained along the way. You know how it would be if he really does have the power to heal — so many people are hopelessly ill. I guess the crowds literally throng him everywhere he goes."

"Do you suppose he will ever come here to our village?"

"Who knows?"

"Well, finish the story. You say the ruler's little girl died before the healer got to her — and he raised her from the dead?"

"That's just what he did! And she got right up and began walking and playing around as though nothing at all had been the matter with her."

All around the room the women gasped and exclaimed, and some of them were sure the healer had to be a prophet of the Lord God.

"But the most amazing thing about it," the narrator went on, "was that this healer made them all promise — the little girl's family, that is — that they would say not one word about what he had done!"

"What a strange man he must be!" the middle-aged woman said.

"Why on earth would he want to keep it a secret? A thing as marvelous as that!"

"Maybe to protect himself," the older woman answered. "After all, if it got around, the poor man could be worn out by people bringing their sick and afflicted to him for healing."

"I wonder what his name is."

"Yes, so do I."

"Bringing a dead child back to life!"

"Yes, just think of it."

The women fell silent again, and some of them stopped

sewing and sat looking out the window down the dusty, winding road that led to Capernaum.

"Wouldn't it be wonderful if the healer would come down the road some day to our village?" one of them breathed.

"Who's that woman running this way? Something must be wrong or she wouldn't be hurrying like that."

"Do you recognize her? I don't."

"Neither do I."

"Look! She's left the road and is walking this way toward the house."

The ladies crowded toward the open doorway, and in a moment one of them shouted: "Veronica! It's Veronica!"

The young woman coming with a light step up the path, her shoulders erect, her head high, was smiling. "Hello," she called, and then, with both hands out toward them, she ran the last few steps to the house. "It's Veronica. Do you remember me? I've come back to help sew. I've come as fast as I could. The first thing I thought about after I was healed yesterday was — now I can come back and help make garments for the poor and afflicted!"

The women stood staring at her. Her cheeks glowed with health; when last any of them had seen her, she was white and frail, her eyes sunken and dark circled.

"You don't even recognize me, do you?" the young woman laughed. "I'm not a ghost! I'm healed. The Master healed me. He cautioned me to say that my faith healed me. But, oh, my faith is in Him — in *Him*."

Finally, the ladies broke their silence, hugged and kissed her, and brought her inside to tell them the whole story. All at once they were telling her that only a few minutes ago they had been wondering about her — wondering even if she might be dead by now from her dreadful hemorrhaging.

"Tell us, my dear! oh, tell us everything that happened!"

"Start from the beginning!"

170

"Well," the bright-eyed young woman said, sitting on the edge of her chair, "I had heard about Jesus of Nazareth, the Master, for a long time."

"Jesus?"

"Yes. His name is Jesus. He is a Galilean, and He is sent from God. For weeks I had heard that all over Capernaum He had been opening blind eyes, causing the deaf to hear, and healing all manner of diseases. I knew, oh, I knew with all my heart that if I could only get near Him — if I could only touch the hem of His garment, He would heal me too. Everything else had failed. We had no more money for doctors, and even if we had, all the doctors were only making me worse. For twelve long years I had not stopped bleeding once! Every new remedy I tried, I was sure would be the right one — nothing was. I had given up. I had accepted the fact of my death, and I am only thirty-two years old. My dear husband had given up too; had reconciled himself to my death as I had.

"And then I heard that Jesus was coming to town. Suddenly, I knew I would not die — not, that is, if by some means I could get near Him. Of course, you all know that Levitically, I was unclean. I had hidden myself for so long; I felt like a leper. I would have to find some way to slip up close enough to touch Him; I could not make my disease known. I was too weak, too distraught to bear any more humiliation. My family thought it foolish for me to go, so I had to sneak out of the house, down the street, and into the enormous crowd around Him. The closer I got, the more certain I was that one touch would heal — even me. And when I saw His head above the crowd — just the back of His head — I knew." She clasped her hands. "I knew I would be healed. Oh, the press of the sick and lame and blind around the Master was dreadful! And it was hot. I found myself pitying Him. He must have been so weary. With strength I haven't had for

171

years, I managed to push my way — literally elbowing — through that terrible crowd, until — until without even having seen His face yet — I managed to stretch my arm around an old, hunchbacked man — and I touched the hem of His garment!"

There was only silence in the room as she spoke now, almost in a whisper, reliving the shining moment.

"Just the hem of His tunic with the tips of my fingers, and — " Still more light came into her face, "and I felt, I really *felt* health flood through my spent body! *I knew I had been healed.*"

The women gasped, and one of them wanted to know if He spoke to her, if He even knew she was there.

"Yes," she went on. "I heard Him turn to one of His disciples and ask who had touched Him. I thought the disciple was a bit sharp with Him. He said something like, 'Well, Master, with a crowd like this, how could anyone know about one person? Everybody's touching You!' And then the Master said He had felt virtue go out of Him. I know now that all the time He knew it was I. He only made mention of it because He knew I needed His special message for me."

"A special message for *you?*"

"Yes," she said, "a special word just for me."

"Well, what was it? What did He say?"

"You see, He knew I needed to learn right away that I never need to be ashamed again, and so He turned and looked at me with the most loving eyes I've ever seen in my entire life, and said: 'Daughter, your faith has made you well; go in peace, and be healed of your disease.' "

* * * * * * * * * *

172   The Gospel account closes with these words: "The woman, knowing what had been done to her, came in fear and trembling and fell down before him, and told him the whole truth."

I doubt that the depth of this simple story will ever be fully explored by anyone. Part, at least, of what God seems to be saying to women today through this remarkable, brief incident — a healing performed on the way to a healing — must have to do with God's infinite knowledge of each one of us as human beings. I have no doubt but that God still heals today. I do not understand why some persons are not healed, but I *know* from experience that many are. (Of course, God is healing when surgery or medical help of any kind is given.) Actually, as I have written this story, I have kept in contact with "the hem of His garment" for myself. In two days I must leave on a hectic autographing trip to Atlanta, Georgia. The way I felt last night when I went to bed, my common sense told me that I had been — since dinner — attacked by some species of "bug." About mid-morning today, when I had finished an urgent stack of mail, my temptation was to declare: "I don't feel up to writing today. If I'm to be ready to leave for Atlanta, I'd better go to bed." Now, I am a firm believer in doctors, medicine, and bed rest. Still, something kept nudging me back to the typewriter. If I am going to write about the woman with the issue of blood, why not experience what I am writing firsthand? So, I began to work. I am within a page or two of being finished now — about mid-afternoon — and I feel almost well. My theory about this matter of direct healing is that we just don't, under ordinary circumstances, know how to direct our faith sufficiently toward God. I know this is true of me. Today, because I was actually writing about a healing, I was better able to direct my own faith.

But what I think He is saying to us in this episode is not necessarily about physical healing. I have been struck this time through the woman's story with the *infinite knowing* of God. *He knew this young woman.* Knew not only her prime need, but knew about her long years of feeling unclean, of being humiliated in public; knew also

173

that *if*, with her particular personality, she got any idea that she was healed by having touched His clothing, she could possibly go off the deep end into superstition and nothing more. He knew also that unless and until she told someone the whole story — stopped keeping it pent-up inside her — her mind would not be able to follow her body into health. And so, because this Teacher — this Healer *was* God, He moved within her heart so that, of her own will, she ". . . told him the whole truth."

Now, by our standards today, there is nothing shameful about hemorrhaging. Weakening, often painful, harrowing — but not shameful. Social mores were different then. Jesus knew how this woman's personality had been twisted by having felt herself a social outcast for twelve years. He wanted her to be perfectly whole. He knew her as she was.

He knew her as she was.

He knows us as we are, and this is why I shy away from "spiritual techniques" set out by one person for another to follow. They can turn quickly into mere superstitions. I shy away from faith-building techniques, from prayer techniques, from group techniques, from healing techniques.

It is well to shy away from any method designed to "reach God." God is already available to everyone — firsthand. It is well, conversely, not to discount *any means* of reaching Him. All we really need to know is that He already knows each one of us inside and out, and He has seen to it that all barriers blocking our contact with Him have been knocked down. This woman's *faith* made her whole. She had no planned approach. She just went to Jesus and touched *Him*.

the Woman with
a crippled back

...bigotry and faith

the Woman with a crippled back

...bigotry and faith

Rather than passing through Samaria, since the prejudice there against the Jews inevitably slowed their journey, Jesus and His men usually traveled through Peraea on their way from Galilee to Judea. It was restful walking and working through the picturesque countryside of rural Peraea. The people thronged about Him, of course, but they were simpler, less sophisticated people than in Jerusalem. The Peraeans were, mainly, country folk with open minds and hearts, who found faith easier.

But just as faith comes more freely to those with uneducated minds, if their hearts are open to it, ignorance can also breed bigotry, and more often than not, the rulers of the small town synagogues in Peraea were bombastic, arrogant, highly prejudiced men. No more vicious in their heckling of Jesus than the cultivated, learned synagogue rulers in the bigger cities, but their anger was more uncouth, and they were less effective in their goading.

In one Peraean village, the heavy-jowled ruler of the synagogue, when he heard that Jesus would be teaching there on the Sabbath, must have girded himself for battle. Undoubtedly, he had encountered the Master before, had

177

felt His authority, had listened to His teaching, and had, of course, utterly missed the point. The provincial ruler had his hackles up. On this particular Sabbath, he would permit no nonsense from this Teacher. He would show who was in charge. Tell those highfalutin, blasphemous parables in his synagogue, would He? He'd show Him once and for all. Of course, he'd have to permit Him to teach, but if there was the slightest sign that He meant to break the Sabbath by healing anyone in this congregation, he'd let Him know how things really stood!

It was a soft spring day, and the air was sweet with the blossoms of the fruit trees that grew everywhere in the valley below the mountain. Each tree was in motion with bees at work, and as the people walked toward the synagogue, they were buzzing together too. The very air was expectant.

The ruler, his thick body perspiring more from resentment and nervousness than from the warm spring day, welcomed Jesus brusquely, showed Him to His seat in the synagogue, and when the time came, motioned for Him to teach. Why did he feel so insecure when the Master was around? Why did His presence make him break out into a cold sweat and all but tremble with rage? He felt clumsier than ever today, more frustrated, and when he glanced over the assembled congregation and saw that *she* had come, he grew even more angry. There she stood — unable to sit down — her thin back so bent she could see nothing but the ground. How long had it been since this faithful member of his synagogue had stood erect, able to see what everyone else took for granted — the sky overhead, the branches of trees, a human face? At least eighteen years, he supposed, and yet she came every Sabbath and worshiped God. He hadn't really dared hope she would stay at home today. A person with a crippled arm might hide it. This woman could never hide herself. And before the ruler had settled himself to endure the

178

teaching of this Man he so resented, so suspected of blasphemy against the Lord God, the worst was happening. The Master had seen the woman with the crippled back standing — bent double — about halfway up a side aisle, and He was calling to her, asking her to come to the front of the room!

The furious ruler's cheeks puffed in and out as his anger made it harder and harder to breathe. She was shuffling down the aisle of the synagogue, only the back of her neck and her twisted shoulders in sight, but she was on her way. The Teacher waited in silence until she reached His side, and then, in a quiet voice, but clear enough for everyone to hear, He said: "Woman, you are freed from your infirmity."

No one moved or made a sound. Not even the woman, who stood, still bent double, staring at the stone floor.

And then, without another word, He laid His hands on her bony, crippled back, and the gasps and exclamations of the people echoed around the high-ceilinged room as the woman, who had not stood erect for eighteen years, lifted herself to her full height and looked into Jesus' face.

Bedlam broke over the congregation, and the people rose to their feet to praise God and rejoice at what happened to the woman they had respected and pitied for so long. The woman who now stood straight, with both hands in the air, was also praising God.

What little control the country ruler possessed was gone. He leaped to his feet, but not to praise God. Over the shouting and the rejoicing, he yelled at the top of his voice: "Listen to me! There are six days on which work ought to be done. Come on those days and be healed — not on the Sabbath! Do you hear me? Come on one of those six days — not on the Sabbath!"

No one heard him, but he kept on berating the people and didn't stop until Jesus spoke again: "You hypocrites! Does not each of you on the Sabbath untie his ox or his

179

ass from the manger, and lead it away to water it? And ought not this woman, a daughter of Abraham whom Satan bound for eighteen years, be loosed from this bond on the Sabbath day?"

The ruler tried again, but the crowd was growing quiet, and it was too humiliating to go on shouting. The Master was going to teach after all, and so, his fat face flushed, his hands trembling, the ruler sank back into his chair, put to shame by the logic of what Jesus had said.

* * * * * * * * * *

We have looked at this incident in the country synagogue from the viewpoint of the inept, prejudiced ruler. Not to belittle him, but to suggest, perhaps, that we today (both men and women) need to realize how our experiences with God influence those around us.

I am speaking here of far more than what we think of as a "Christian witness." Actually, we are considering a totally different thing. And the reason I feel it is important for us to begin to think about this is so that we will become more realistic in our judgments of people.

If something especially good happens — a physical or spiritual or mental healing, or a set of knotty circumstances untangled — we, if we love Him, praise God. Among our friends, relatives, and acqaintances there will be those with peace *and* love in their own hearts, who, like most of the people in the synagogue congregation that day, will rejoice with us. But there will be also those, who, like the bigoted, shallow-thinking ruler, are so afraid of someone else's victories, so insecure in themselves, so fearful of being proven wrong, will rage at us. This poor man, the ruler of the synagogue, was not capable of trying to trick Jesus with cleverly devised questions, as were some of the more sophisticated rulers in Jerusalem and elsewhere, but he could still rage when the good woman was healed, and he did.

180

I well remember during the early days of my own Christian life when I was criticized because my conversion had filled me with joy. "Too much joy" for the Bible teacher who accused me of "hamming it up" because she had never known the same kind of joy in her own life. New Christians are frequently "hams." It is all so new and so exciting, there is the immature tendency to dramatize one's own experience with God. I'm sure I did. But I *was* immature. And happily, I had read about this embittered small-town ruler. I didn't have to be hurt or even be confused by the "Christian leader" who dressed me down so sharply.

What I am really saying is that we all need to develop sensitivity to other people. Even after you have matured in Christ, there will still be times when your praising God for some kindness will strike someone else the wrong way. The same God who dispensed the kindness in the first place can give needed sensitivity.

Peter's wife

...who inspired her husband

Peter's wife

...who inspired her husband

"We will die well if we remember the Lord," Peter said, as he sat in the cell beside his aging wife in Mamertine Prison in Rome, almost forty years after the crucifixion of Jesus. "We will both die well, if we will but remember how He died."

She laid her hand on Peter's and whispered, "Yes, my husband. If we remember how the Lord died — *and* that He is risen again forever."

The old man managed a smile. "Yes. You have always kept me thinking straight, haven't you, my dear? Always. Through every year of our lives together, I have been blessed beyond any man. Even during the years before I began to follow the Master, you were patient with me. How did you come by such inner strength? Before I met the Lord — before Pentecost, in fact — your husband was the most difficult of men. High-strung, pigheaded, impulsive — hard to live with. And yet you have made every hour good."

185

"I have loved you."

He put his big arm around her. "Yes, you have loved me. And I have never deserved it. Just as I do not deserve to be crucified as my Lord was crucified!" He got up, rubbing his gray head, and paced the damp stone floor of the cell. "I am not afraid to die. I know I will go at once to be *with* Him again. Just think of it! We will be where we can *see* His face. But I cannot — I will not be crucified as He was. That I could not endure."

She went to him and turned him around so that he had to look at her. "Peter, listen to me — just once more. Dying will not be easy for either of us. You do not believe any more deeply than I that we will be with the Lord again when we die. With all my heart I believe that. And so I, too, am not *afraid* to die. But dying will be no easier than living has been. Glorious, yes, because of Him. But not easy. You will need your strength to die — your inner strength. Let me be practical just one more time. Do not waste your energy by resisting the kind of death you will die, my beloved. The Lord would not want you to do that. He would want you to go bravely, quietly, not resisting — leaving the method to them."

A slow, shamefaced smile broke over Peter's lined face. He leaned down and kissed her on her forehead. "It's no wonder you have been such a good wife. No wonder at all that through those long years when I was away following the Master, you understood. Or, if you didn't understand then, you waited until you did. Suddenly, none of the patience or courage you showed during the years you traveled with me surprises me any longer. At this moment, when we are about to die, I am seeing you as though for the first time. And what I see is a woman filled with the Spirit of God — a woman whose dear body will be — killed, but — " His old eyes filled suddenly with tears, and he took her in his arms.

186   "Do not weep, Peter. Our old bodies have served their purpose anyway. It is such a comfort to know we will go to Him together. Do not weep!"

He led her to the stone bench again, and they both sat

down wearily. After a while he said, "Perhaps God is giving me this clear sight of you during our last hour together. Perhaps I have been too occupied with my own life with Him to have seen you — shining beside me. Oh, I have always loved you. I used you as an example when writing to the churches — an example of what a woman of God should be. Your beauty had never been merely the outward adorning of your hair or the wearing of gold and expensive robes. It has been the hidden person of the heart — the imperishable jewel of a gentle and quiet spirit. I have seen you and have loved you, but never as now. I draw strength from you — now."

"If I have had a gentle and quiet spirit, Peter, it has been because of the life of the Lord within me. Do you remember how gentle and quiet He was when He used to come to our house?"

"Yes. Gentle and quiet — but always so strong. I can still feel the strength of His presence in your mother's room the night He healed her, can't you?"

"Yes, and the strength of His smile as He watched her hustling around minutes later — serving Him, seeing to His every need. He had strength even in His smile, didn't He?"

"Even in His smile, my dear."

They sat for a long time in silence, and then Peter turned to her. "It is almost time. I will go on loving you forever."

"And I will love you forever, too, Peter. I wonder how long we'll be apart today? An hour? A moment?"

"The Lord told that thief on the cross beside Him that they would be together *that* day in paradise." Suddenly, the old man's face clouded. "Oh, if *only* I had gone with Him to His death! Why did I run? *Why did I run?*"

187

"Peter!" She put her hand over his mouth. "This is not the time to waste your energy on regret. You have been forgiven. He will never mention any of that to you again.

We are going to live with Him forever, and not once will He ever permit you to think about any of that."

He smiled a little. "Of course. You're right as usual. Thank you for reminding me."

The outer door of the prison clanked shut, and the clump of heavy boots and armor rang and echoed down the vaulted stone corridor outside their cell. They stood up, holding hands, their eyes fixed on the barred door.

"We will die well, Peter, if we remember the Lord."

"Yes," he breathed, his old shoulders straight. "Remember the Lord, my wife. Remember the Lord."

* * * * * * * * * *

According to Herbert Lockyer,* there is a poignant legend in church tradition which tells of Peter and his wife dying together, and that says he comforted her with the words, "Remember the Lord." This, of course, is not in the Scripture, but the idea appeals to me strongly, and I have based the vignette on it. The actual setting is not important, I suppose, but what we can learn from it is.

Very little is written in the New Testament about Peter's wife. We are not even told her name, and yet she is there in the background of the life of the big fisherman whom Jesus loved. What I'd like to emphasize about her here is her undeniable elasticity of spirit. If Peter was using his own wife as the example of what he felt a truly Christian woman should be, the two words "quiet" and "gentle" give us our clue to her ability to adapt without complaining — to be elastic.

A look at Peter's stormy life shows instantly how much his wife would *need* to adapt. First, during the early years of their marriage, before Peter (then Simon) met the Master, Mrs. Simon undoubtedly had to contend with a hotheaded, impetuous, unpredictable man. Even after Simon met Jesus, he remained unpredictable. He was an

188

* *Women of the Bible* (Zondervan)

extremist. He leaped without thinking. Remember the stormy night when he and the other disciples saw Jesus coming toward them on the water? Who jerked off his clothes and jumped overboard into the water — trying to walk on it too? Peter. And, of course, who began to sink for lack of faith? Peter. He could not have been an easy man with whom to live. Lovable, I'm sure. But not easy to love steadily, day in and day out. Only a woman with an elastic, adaptable nature could have managed. Especially when her mother lived with them. But somehow, Peter's wife did manage, not only through the chaotic years when, seeming to have deserted her, he left home to follow Jesus, but later too.

After the Lord's death and resurrection and return to His Father's house, Peter, filled then with the Holy Spirit — more stable, more emotionally mature, less prone to ups and downs, spent the remainder of his years traveling and preaching the Gospel of the Lord he worshiped. No easy life for the woman who loved him, but she went too, according to Paul in I Corinthians 9:5.

Peter was stronger, kinder, more poised after Pentecost, but elasticity on her part was still required. Not weak submissiveness merely, but the kind of elasticity that is undergirded by true strength. There can be no *gentleness* of heart without elasticity. If a woman is furious at her husband for being unpredictable, her fury doesn't show up in *gentleness,* nor *quietness* of heart. And Peter's own description of a true Christian woman contained both words. I strongly suspect his wife inspired them.

189

the Widow and her copper coins

...one penny was everything

the Widow and her copper coins

...one penny was everything

It was Paschal week, and from all over the known world, Jews were streaming into Jerusalem. Women worked long hours in their kitchens preparing food for the Passover Feast — baking loaves and loaves of unleavened bread and stacks of unleavened cakes to be dipped in the slow-simmered sweet sauce. Children and old men and women gathered the bitter herbs — lettuce and endive — to remind them all of the bitter bondage of Egypt from which God had freed His people. And into the Temple all day long during this holy week streamed the rich and the poor to drop their sacrificial gifts into the Temple treasury — containers lining the low wall of the Women's Court in the Temple.

Both men and women could enter the Women's Court, and so Jesus had been teaching there on the day the crowds were extremely heavy. In the afternoon He sat apart, alone, on the low Temple wall, watching the people come with their gifts, deposit them in one of the large urns, and depart. His time was growing short to be among them as one of them. The Son of Man knew this because He was also the Son of God, and so He sat watch-

193

ing the people He had come to save — watching them and thinking about them as they came and went.

He watched the rich and the very rich, dressed in silks and tasseled garments, their servants carrying their offerings until the moment the money was to be placed in the holy urns. Some of the wealthy made their offerings quietly, unobtrusively, but not many, He noticed. Most of them at least cleared their throats loudly just as the gold dropped. Some even lifted the gift high in the air and then tossed it with a flourish into the sacred coffers. The moderately well-off came, and the poor and the very poor. Almost no one noticed the poor, but they came; some ashamed of the pittance they placed before the Lord God; others seeming to drop in their coins without any reaction at all.

In an unusually large press of people crowding across the wide stone pavement of the Women's Court, Jesus saw one lone woman making her way to the urn a few yards from where He sat. She was of medium height, perhaps in her sixties, her widow's garments well-patched but thin from much washing and long years of wear. She did not try to elbow her way through the crowd, nor did she sneak through, ashamed as some of the others had been. This woman simply walked steadily toward the urn, moving this way and that as other people pushed past her, but she neither hurried nor loitered. Some surreptitiously counted out their money as they approached the treasury wall, but she didn't. Her mind was made up, her gift in her hand, and so she reached the urn, dropped in two copper coins — "which make a penny" — bowed her head a moment, and walked back across the court toward the Temple gate.

194   Jesus watched her go, looked around in the crowd for His disciples, and motioned for them to join Him. "Truly, I say to you," He said thoughtfully, "this poor widow has put in more than all those who are contributing to the

treasury." He gestured toward the rich and the very rich, making a scene of their heavy bags of gold thudding into the bronze urns. "For they all contributed out of their abundance; but she out of her poverty has put in everything she had, her whole living."

＊ ＊ ＊ ＊ ＊ ＊ ＊ ＊ ＊ ＊

Enough has been written about the intrinsic value of the widow's mite from the standpoint of the stewardship of our worldly goods. As Jesus so clearly saw, she *had* given all she owned. ". . . her whole living." She hadn't saved back enough for bread or thread or oil. It was a pittance — two copper coins worth one penny — but her gift shone brightly in His eyes because He knew what the giving had cost her.

It seems to me that we, as women (men too), could gain by looking beneath this valid, but more obvious interpretation down to the deepest possible meaning of what Jesus said concerning the widow's gift, of His *reaction* to her gift.

He had been watching people come and go with their large and small offerings for several minutes without seeing anything He felt important enough to mention to His disciples. Suddenly, as though He were startled by the woman's gift, He called them. Had she done something almost no one ever does? Oh, we may think we're entering into real self-denial — we often inconvenience ourselves for God's sake — but does anyone really do what this woman did so that God, seeing all there is to see about everyone, makes a point of it? Reacts in His heart with joy over it?

We are not now speaking of giving money or clothing or even of our time and energies in service to other people. I think we will profit more from this woman's story if we look deeply into our inner selves and take some measurements of what might be our real or imagined self-denials

— some measurements of our true righteousness, not imagined righteousness.

Look at our habits, for example. If you have never been by nature a gossip, is it an act of self-denial that you don't gossip now? Should you feel righteous? If you have never had a drink of alcohol — can't imagine that you'd really like it, or if you've tried and know you don't, is this self-denial that you don't drink habitually? An alcoholic who does not drink *is* giving of his very way of life. With him or with her, it *is* a giving up. He or she can praise God and experience righteousness because a deep, agonizing effort has been involved.

I will use myself as an example. When I sit at my typewriter for six or seven hours, hard at work on a novel or a non-fiction book such as this one, my back begins to ache, my arms grow weary, my body longs for exercise. I am just plain tired, sometimes really wrung out. There is always a certain inner agony that is part of any creating. But, should I make a big deal of it? Should I feel proud to the degree that I go about telling everyone how hard I worked today? How long I dutifully sat at my typewriter? Should I go about slyly seeking a little sympathy for my aching shoulders? Of course not! I love to write. In fact, I'm restless and not nearly as pleasant when I'm not working on a book. There is absolutely no sacrifice involved whatever. I even make a fairly decent living writing books, so why should I feel more virtuous than any other human being who has simply put in a good day's work? *But,* if I sit at the typewriter for the same length of time, pounding just as hard, thinking just as deeply while answering mail all day, I have some small reason to feel clear with God. Not because there is any less value in the manuscripts than there is in the letters, but because when I write books, I'm enjoying myself in spite of the hard work. When I answer letter after letter, while some are most interesting, I'm sacrificing a little. Giving up

196

time from what I'd much rather be doing — writing books.

It is also very easy (too easy, I think) for me to trust people. Like my father, I tend to be too lenient, too quick to expect the best from persons I don't know. Like him, also, I'm always sure something good is just up ahead. Life has increased my realism considerably, but I'm a born optimist. So, am I to feel righteous, of great faith, simply because by nature I'm *not* a cynic? A doubting Thomas?

If you pity your husband's best friend because the poor man is obviously henpecked by a sharp-tongued wife, and if you know for a fact that your husband is not, and you know that he is not because you *hate* quarrels and arguments — should you be reveling in self-denial? Is it any effort for you not to nag him when you hate to nag?

As always, everything Jesus said holds layer upon layer of meaning — enough to cover all our needs. In the story of the poor widow with her two mites, I believe He is saying far more than that we should give generously of our money. What may be sacrificial for me may not be at all for you. What may constitute genuine self-denial for you may not require anything at all of me. Only He knows us as we really are.

the Syro-Phoenician woman

...she met his challenge

the Syro-Phoenician woman

...she met his challenge

Jesus and His disciples had just entered the outskirts of the ancient Phoenician city of Tyre on the Mediterranean. They had walked twenty miles since daylight; the sun had gone down back of the lofty Lebanon range behind the city; He was tired and needed rest from the crowds of people who had followed Him most of the day. He had looked forward to reaching Tyre, because there were friends there, purple dye-makers, whose comfortable home overlooked the beaches where the special mollusks from which Tyrian dye was made were gathered daily. Jesus was always welcome at their home, for they were His followers, and looked for Him every time they heard He was in the region of Tyre and its neighboring city, Sidon.

His host had just washed the Lord's feet; His hostess had brought leben and fruit, when into the house burst a strange woman, a Syro-Phoenician by birth, who fell breathless at Jesus' feet, crying out in Greek, "Have mercy on me, O Lord, Son of David; my daughter is severely possessed by a demon!"

For a moment, the woman kept her head to the floor,

201

but when Jesus said nothing in reply, she cried again, "Have mercy! Have mercy!"

Her begging grew so intense that His disciples could stand it no longer. "Send her away, Lord! Send her away! She is crying after us, so that You must send her away! How can we rest with all this noise going on?"

He looked at the men, not at the weeping woman, and said matter-of-factly, "I was sent only to the lost sheep of the house of Israel."

The men nodded in pious agreement, scowling at the Canaanite woman who, after another long, awkward moment, raised her head and said, "Lord, help me!"

Still looking past her, Jesus answered firmly, "It is not fair to take the children's bread and throw it to the dogs."

The room crackled with tension. They had never heard Him speak this way to anyone. His host and the disciples exchanged glances, wondering what the Master would say next.

But the woman herself spoke again, her voice quiet, strong, reasonable, deliberate. "Yes, Lord, yet even the dogs eat the crumbs that fall from their master's table."

He looked directly at her now, studied her face for a while, and answered, "O woman, great is your faith! Be it done for you as you desire."

Without wondering at His hesitancy, the woman ran from the house, out through the courtyard, and down the road to her own home. He had not moved from the couch on which He reclined when she had begged His mercy, and yet she found her little daughter in her bed, asleep — the demon gone.

*   *   *   *   *   *   *   *   *

202   For a long, long time this story about the poor Canaanite mother, who asked only that her afflicted child be healed, puzzled me. After I wrote the vignette portion of this chapter just now, I looked back into the pages of the

very first Bible I used after my own conversion, and sure enough, I had written in the margin: "I don't understand this one at all!" In another Bible, some ten or fifteen years later, in the margin beside the Matthew account, there is simply a question mark. Someone once said that reading the Bible was much like eating a fish. The parts we can't digest — the bones — we stack on the side of our plate. I will go a bit further than that: The parts we can't *now* understand, we stack to one side for *later*. The light of the Spirit of God keeps shining, and when we are alert and ready (and free of our prejudices) our understanding opens.

The story of the pathetic Syro-Phoenician woman is one of the passages I've waited to understand. I now see this much anyway: Jesus was not, as it might seem, showing racial prejudice toward her. Do you know, I've heard prejudiced people say that He was? Anyone who has read the detailed account of His meeting with the woman at the well of Jacob in Samaria knows He was not capable of racial discrimination. Anyone who knows *Him* at all, knows this.

What was He doing, then? There is no doubt that His words *sounded* rude, superior, even insensitive. "I was sent only to the lost sheep of the house of Israel." She was a pagan Syro-Phoenician woman who did not even speak Aramaic, but Greek. He knew she was not of the house of Israel, so wasn't it rather crude to remind her? When His disciples, feeling smug that they were of the house of Israel, and therefore specially chosen, urged Him to send her away, instead of taking them down a notch as He always did under circumstances like this, He seemed to grow still more aloof, more cruel toward the weeping woman. "It is not fair," He said, "to take the children's bread and throw it to the dogs." Even this did not daunt her. She simply reminded Him that at least the dogs under the master's table were permitted to eat the crumbs.

203

She was asking only one small thing of Him — one crumb.

When He seemed suddenly to do a complete turnabout, not only by healing her daughter from a distance, but praising her faith, what was He intending *us* to understand? Had He been giving an object lesson to His disciples? Had He merely been testing this woman's faith? Both, perhaps. Still, there seems to be more than this. Obviously this woman was exhausted, heartbroken, near despair over the pitiable condition of her little girl. Undoubtedly she had spent night after night with the tormented child, trying vainly to protect her from her imagined fears, trying to guard her from her own inner struggles — trying, perhaps, to keep the child from destroying herself. Jesus could see that the mother had borne all she could bear. Her trouble exceeded that of most women. Was He, by seeming to put her off, seeming to turn a deaf ear to her pleas, telling us that even though our hearts are broken, our lives choked with trouble and sorrow, our resources at an end — He is still there? Is He saying, "Exercise your faith in Me, even when I appear not to notice your tears"?

Could He be saying that we are not to believe God has deserted us because trouble keeps arriving in torrents? Whatever He is saying, it is not an easy thing, but it is God Himself saying it, and for those of us who claim to have put our eternal faith in Him, it should be enough that He is speaking.

There will always be mysteries concerning God which we cannot fully understand during our earthly journey. I do not understand all His parables; I do not understand about miracles; I do not understand all His teaching. But our faith is not to be placed in these — it is safe only when it is placed in the One who *lived love* before us right here on our planet — *as* one of us.

204

the Woman
taken in adultery

...she waited with him

the Woman taken in adultery

...she waited with him

They jerked and dragged her along the dusty ground toward the place outside the Temple enclosure where Jesus was teaching. Her matted hair hung over her eyes. Her dress was soiled, ripped, and wrinkled. She was young, in her twenties, and in spite of the shame and fear, she was beautiful. Two officers held her bruised arms, twisted them, as they forced the woman through the crowd, her short, sharp cries turning the people's attention from Jesus to stare at her. Prancing at the front of the small procession of priests accompanying her was the young priest who had spearheaded the efforts to trap Jesus. Aware that there was now another trap being set, the Master stood in silence while the odd little company came nearer. His heart moved toward the woman as her accusers shoved her to the very center of the gaping crowd, directly in front of Him.

"Teacher," the scheming priest said in mock outrage, "we need your help! This woman has been caught in the very act of adultery. Now, Moses ordered in the law to stone such as she. What do you say, Teacher?"

Jesus looked at the priest, then at the wretched young

207

woman who stood with her head down. The curious crowd shoved and jostled, trying to get a better look at her.

"Who is she?" they muttered. "Can you see who she is?"

"What do you say, Teacher?" The priest pressed his question.

Jesus glanced back at him again, but said nothing.

One of the officers holding the woman twisted her arm sharply so that she cried out. The people nearest her made a more determined effort to see her face.

And then a surprising thing happened. The Master, after looking for a long moment from one to another in the crowd and in the little band of priests and soldiers, stooped down, quite casually, and began to write in the dust on the ground.

For a moment there was only silence. Some of the people stood on tiptoe trying to see what He was writing. The priests and the scribes stared at one another, their faces blank. When the crowd began to titter and laugh, the officiating priest attempted to fill the awkward silence.

He took one step toward Jesus. "Well? What do you say, Teacher? I believe you know the law well, and since you do, you are aware that Moses ordered in the law that a woman like this one is to be stoned. What do you say? *What do you say?*"

Slowly, Jesus stood up and again studied the accusing men. Some of them shuffled their feet uneasily; others coughed and grew red in the face; still others looked even more arrogant.

The Lord was in no hurry to speak. He seemed determined to wait until the crowd had grown utterly silent. Then He said in a strong, clear voice: "Let him who is without sin among you be the first to throw a stone at her."

208 Directly, He stooped down again and resumed writing with His finger in the dust.

Now, no one even coughed. One of the officers who had been gripping the young woman's arm let go. No one spoke. What was there to say? Without risking so much as a glance at each other, one by one the accusers, led by the young priest, turned and hurried away. The remaining officer, who had already released the woman, gaped at Jesus for a moment, then ran. Like a great, silent wave, the crowd moved back out of the Temple grounds.

Jesus was left alone with the woman.

In a moment, He looked up and asked quietly, "Woman, where are they? Has no one condemned you?"

For the first time she lifted her head to look at Him. "No one, Lord," she whispered.

"Neither do I condemn you." His voice was gentle, but firm. "Go, and do not sin again."

* * * * * * * * * *

In an earlier book* I find I wrote this comment following the scriptural record of the forgiveness of the woman taken in adultery:

> This is one of the most telling stories in any of the Gospel accounts. Two things strike me: Jesus did not stand around posturing, attempting to look and act like Someone special. I have read that other authors feel He must have written something profound in the dirt at His feet. I doubt that. Of course, it wouldn't change anything for us if He did, but I think He was *doodling.* Much as one of us would doodle while waiting for some boring, dull tirade to end. He knew perfectly well that the scribes and Pharisees had brought the wretched adulteress to Him, not to make certain that her punishment was just, but to trap *Him.* He knew everything the old boys were going to say, knew their tricky motives, knew their tired old logic. *Only the woman was important to Him.* He knew *she* could be redeemed. They could not be, as long as they stayed locked up in their precious status quo. He stooped down and doodled on the ground for a while, as though hoping they would go away. When

209

* *Learning To Live From The Gospels* (Lippincott)

they didn't, He straightened up and said something that would send them scurrying while there was time. And then He used the whole incident redemptively. Not only to forgive the woman's sins, but to point out once more that the Son of God did not come to condemn. One more thing that comes to me, which I have never thought of before, is that she waited.

And this is what I feel that we, as women, should think about. Why did the woman wait? Why didn't she run away too? Both her guards left. She could have - run. Why didn't she? Wasn't she as guilty in her own heart as the men who did hurry off?

Yes, she was guilty. If she hadn't been, if they had been accusing her unjustly, Jesus would not have told her to "go and sin no more." He did say that to her, and so we can be sure the girl had been caught in the very act of adultery. The men ran because of their guilt, so why did she wait — alone with Jesus?

I feel it was because *she* meant Him no harm. She had sinned, but her sin was the sin of twisted love. The scribes and priests had sinned too, but their sin was the sin of self-righteousness. Hunger drove her to her sin. Greed drove them to theirs. It has been said that the most redeemable person alive is the one who has sinned *seeking love*. Whether this is true or not, there is food for much thought here. In no way did Jesus condone her sin. Sin is sin. But He saw in her what He did not see in her accusers. In her, He saw the hunger for real love, for joy, for giving. In them, He saw the lust for power, the inevitable brutality of self-righteousness. They were bending their sharp intellects to trap Him. She was, if she had only known it before, seeking Him because she was seeking love.

210

She waited, I believe, because standing before Him, she saw not only the sin in her own life, but the hope for her in His.

Her accusers left because they had to. Jesus did not reject them. They rejected Him.

She waited because she had to wait. He did not urge her to stay. He did not take her hand and talk to her about her soul. He was just there as He was. She was there as she was — ready and open to receive His forgiveness, as He was ready and eager to forgive.

It has ever been an amazement to me that respectable church people are almost always quicker to condemn a woman who has committed adultery than they are to condemn a man or woman who ignores Christian ethics to live by trickery.

the Mother of
the blind son

. . . "he is of age, ask him"

the Mother of the blind son

... "he is of age, ask him"

The very next day after her son's eyes had been opened so that, for the first time in his life, he could see her face, her neighbors came crowding into her house. Some of them had thought up excuses to come, such as the need to borrow a little meal or oil, but most of them came frankly to know exactly what had happened.

"It seems to me you're being very peculiar about all this," one of the women said. "A person would think you'd be praising the Lord today!"

"I am praising the Lord," the unwilling hostess declared, her face a careful mask. "Why wouldn't a mother be rejoicing in her heart when her only son, who has been blind from birth, can now see?"

"Well, that's what we thought," another neighbor said, her head to one side, scrutinizing the mother. "That's what we all thought."

The woman drew closer to where the woman sat, dressed in her best clothing, seeming both to resent and welcome the burst of attention she was receiving in her community.

"Tell us exactly what happened! We heard the Master

healed your son's blindness without even being asked to do it. Is this true? Did He?"

"We heard the Teacher spat on the ground and made a kind of paste with the spittle and dust and spread it on your son's eyes. Is this what He really did?"

"It's just what He did," another woman interrupted. "My husband was there. He saw it with his own eyes!"

"Let her tell it. It was her son!"

"Yes, tell us exactly what took place. Every little detail."

The mother sat erect, defensive. "My husband and I were not present when the — miracle took place. My son was sitting where he has always sat by the Temple begging alms. After all, what else could he do to bring in a little money? He was blind!"

"We all know that," a neighbor answered. "We should all know it. We've known your son since his birth, don't forget. But surely the boy has told you the details of exactly how it happened!"

"He told his father too. Your husbands will have gotten the whole story from him by now. Let them tell you. They will anyway."

"Well! You certainly don't act like a woman whose heart is praising the Lord for blessings received."

"I've said my husband and I were not present when the Rabbi opened our son's eyes!"

"But when they took your son before the Pharisees to give them a chance to question him about this strange Teacher from Galilee, you and your husband were called to testify that the boy had been born blind, weren't you?"

"We were called."

"And what did you tell them?"

"The truth, of course. That he had always been blind."

216 "Didn't the Pharisees ask you and your husband to explain how his eyes had been restored?"

"They did."

"Well, what did you tell them?"

"We told them he was our son, that he had been born blind, and that he could now see. What else was there to tell them since we weren't there when it happened?"

"But hadn't your son told you the details of how this strange Teacher had healed him?"

"He had."

"Then why didn't you tell the rulers of the synagogue?"

The mother squirmed on her chair, looked diffident, and said nothing.

"Do you think they want to be put out of the synagogue?" A neighbor answered for her. "I, for one, think they did the right thing. Why, if they had said they knew for a fact that this Rabbi called Jesus had healed their son's eyes in an instant, they would have been confessing that He is of God! Anyone knows the word is that if one of us confesses this, out we go from the congregation of our people. I don't think you should look so uncomfortable, my friend. You and your husband did just the right thing exactly!"

Her hostess smiled slightly, nodded, but her fingers were twisting the hem of her sash.

"I heard this Teacher's disciple had asked Him if your boy's blindness came about because he had sinned or because you and your husband had sinned. Is this true?"

The woman gasped, then studied the mother's face more closely.

"Did they ask that question?"

"I've heard they did," their hostess said, her voice guarded.

"Well, what did the Teacher answer them? Who sinned?"

The boy's mother pulled herself straight again in her chair and declared, "He said no one had sinned!"

"No one? Why, the prophet Isaiah wrote that 'all have sinned and come short of the glory of God!'"

"Don't be stupid," the mother snorted. "What the

217

Teacher said was the boy's blindness was not caused by *our* sin!"

"Oh, I thought all affliction was caused by someone's sin!"

"He says not, but nobody really knows who He is."

"Well," a neighbor sighed, "at least *you've* been vindicated."

"I certainly have been," the mother snapped. "And if you're all going out to gossip, as I'm sure you are, I hope and pray you won't forget to add that!"

"Oh, we won't. We promise. But what *did* you tell the Pharisees when they tried to get you to explain how the boy had been made to see again?"

"My husband and I told them what any sensible parents would tell them. 'He is of age, ask him.' We said that and nothing more."

* * * * * * * * *

Does it seem to you that I have painted this woman as hard and unloving? Think about it. Her son had been born blind, and had, of course, required constant care all during the years in which he was growing up. He was apparently still living with or near his parents as a man, so they must have given him the added care he needed. I don't think they lacked parental interest in their son. I think they lacked courage. Neither the father nor the mother wanted to be put out of the synagogue. They did what they had to do in order to stay in. They tossed the problem at their son. "He is of age, ask him." In one way, they were tired of their burden. He could see again; he was of age; they had done so much for him through the years — let the young man handle this for himself.

They lacked courage and they were utterly human and expedient.

But, to me, there seems to be another subtlety here

218

which we need to notice. Wasn't this mother's own ego involved in her answer? After all, she lived in the era when most Jews believed that all misfortune was the punishment for someone's sin. All through the years she had carried the secret humiliation before her neighbors. She knew they all thought that either she or her husband had done something to have caused their son to be born blind. She couldn't come right out and confess that Jesus was the Christ, but she got in her lick about her own innocence. This was her son, bone of her bone, and it was a relief that the Rabbi also said he had done nothing to cause his affliction. The woman did not take the gift of eternal life from the Lord, but she took His word for it that she was innocent. Of course, this is not what Jesus meant at all. But it was what she wanted to hear. She stopped her ears from that point on.

Mothers still suffer, wondering what people will say when their children do some shocking thing. This isn't the Christian way, but it is the human way. Children want their parents to be charming, presentable, successful. It helps their own stock to be able to boast about mother and father. This isn't necessarily Christian either, but it is human.

So, in this dramatic incident from John's gospel, as with every other incident in which Christ figures, there are many levels of understanding. The bright light of discernment penetrates the very human nature of both parents — of us. They lacked courage; they protected themselves — even at the expense of their son; they took only from Christ what pleased them.

Most of us do not take *all* He offers.

Rhoda

...the slave with a capacity for joy

Rhoda

...the slave with a capacity for joy

In the large, upper front room of the widow Mary's home in Jerusalem, most of the new church had gathered to pray. They met regularly in the house of John Mark's mother, Mary, but tonight there was an urgency in their prayers. Their beloved leader Peter was in jail — arrested by Herod for preaching the risen Christ. One of their number, James the Lesser, had already been martyred. God *had* to protect Peter. The new believers would be lost without him.

It was after midnight, but still the praying went on. No one seemed willing to leave. With the very human mixture of love and anxiety, of faith and fear, the Christians pleaded with the Lord God to spare Peter's life, to free him from prison, to send him back to them.

"If only Barnabas or my son John Mark were here," Mary said, as they rested a moment, giving thanks in their hearts that the Lord was hearing their prayers. "I know no human hand can set our brother, Peter, free, but it would comfort me so if my nephew or my son could pray with us."

"Excuse me, ma'am," her young slave girl, Rhoda, said, sitting on the edge of her chair.

223

"Yes, Rhoda. What is it?"

"Master John Mark and Master Barnabas *are* with us."

"In spirit, I know, Rhoda."

"Oh, more than that, ma'am! The Lord said when two or three are gathered together in His name, He would be right in their midst. Well, we're together and He's here. So, since Master John Mark and Master Barnabas are no doubt together praying too on their evangelistic journey, the Lord is also with them." She grew more excited, her words tumbling out. "So, if the Lord Christ is with them *and* with us, then we are *all* of us together in Him!"

Mary smiled. "You're right, of course, Rhoda. But I think we'd better get back to our praying. I feel I'd like to pray now, if no one minds. I believe it will help quiet my heart." The others nodded assent, knelt with Mary, and she began to talk to God. "Oh, risen Christ! We are here gathered together in Your name. Blessing Your name; praising You for revealing the Father to us; asking that in Your infinite mercy You would bring about the quick, safe release of our brother Peter from his — "

"Listen!" Rhoda jumped to her feet. "Excuse me, ma'am, but someone is knocking on the front door downstairs!"

Without another word, Rhoda ran from the room, down the outside stair, and across the courtyard to the high wooden door.

"Rhoda!" Mary called from the upstairs window. "Rhoda, you foolish girl, take care! Don't you know that could be a trick of Herod's?"

Down in the courtyard, Rhoda pressed her ear against the thick door and listened. There was only the soft, urgent knock again.

"Come back, you crazy slave girl!" One of the believers was shouting now from the upstairs meeting room. "You can be killed and get the rest of us killed as well!"

Rhoda, her ear still at the door, heard the insistent knocking once more. Her heart pounded far faster than the quick rapping at the gate, but she was too excited to listen to the warnings from the meeting upstairs. She *had* to know who was there.

"Who is it?" she whispered. "Will you tell me your name?"

"It is I, Peter! Open the door, Rhoda!"

Her hands flew to her mouth. It was *he*. Their prayers had been answered! Peter, beloved Peter, was no longer in prison. He was standing this minute at the door of the house — free. Free and alive! Without a word to Peter, the girl raced back across the wide courtyard, up the stair, and burst into the room where some of the people had gone back to praying — not only for Peter's safety, but for their own as well.

"He's here! Master Peter is here! He's not in prison any more — he's *here*."

"The girl is mad!"

"She's taken complete leave of her senses!"

"No!" Rhoda shouted, her face glowing with joy. "He's here!"

"Of course, she's mad! Look at that silly smile."

"It is a smile of gladness," the girl protested, whirling around before them in a little joyful dance. "The one we prayed for is down there at the gate knocking to get in!"

They all heard the knock this time, and for a moment, no one spoke.

"See?" Rhoda exclaimed. "He's still knocking! I asked who it was, and the same, familiar voice of Master Peter whispered, 'It is I, Peter! Open the door.' "

"Then why didn't you open it, foolish girl?"

"I — I was too excited, I guess."

"Too feeble-minded, you mean!"

"Why do you say that?" Rhoda demanded. "We all prayed, didn't we?"

"Yes, of course, we prayed, but — "

225

"Then why is it not possible that he is at the gate even now?"

"It must be his guardian angel," someone volunteered.

"It is not an angel," Rhoda declared. "An angel would not stand out there and knock. An angel does not have to have a door opened for him. It is not an angel; it is Master Peter! I heard his voice. The Lord heard our prayers — and when He hears, He answers!"

* * * * * * * * * *

Of course, it *was* Peter knocking at the door of Mary's house. ". . . Peter continued knocking; and when they opened, they saw him and were amazed. But motioning to them with his hand to be silent, he described to them how the Lord had brought him out of prison."

They were all amazed — except Rhoda. Rhoda was full of joy! The random comments of the faithful gathered in the house of Mary of Jerusalem are all too typical. "The girl is crazy!" "It must be his angel!" True, it was a common Jewish belief that every Israelite was given a special guardian angel who resembled him, but Rhoda tossed that theory aside immediately. No angel ever needed to knock on a door in order to gain entrance. An angel could come right through a locked door.

The serving maid, Rhoda, obviously did not have the most organized mind, but she had an enormous capacity for joy — the kind of childlike joy that comes as an inevitable result of childlike faith. There is no indication that Rhoda was surprised to hear Peter's voice. The Scriptures tell us that ". . . in her *joy* she did not open the gate but ran. . . . " Not in her *surprise* — in her *joy*.

Rhoda did *not* use her head (which, of course, could have cost Peter his life), but she did use her faith. Obviously, Mary's slave girl had come to know the living Lord too. There evidently was no segregation in Mary's household — no seeing to it by the mistress that the ser-

226

vants "kept their places." They were all praying together to the Lord God for the safety of the man they loved and needed. Rhoda was with her mistress that night, praying. And — more than anyone else gathered in the spacious upper room of Mary's house — Rhoda believed and expected an answer to their prayers.

The young servant girl's heart had no room for doubt — only expectancy. After all, she was the one who ran downstairs first when Peter knocked. I don't think this is a commentary on Rhoda's mentality. I believe this little incident is included in the Scriptures as a comment on Rhoda's capacity for joy — and perhaps as a commentary on the lack of it among some of the other believers.

I don't really think we need envy Rhoda her somewhat muddled brain, but I do pray for her capacity to be glad.

Mary of Jerusalem

...John Mark's mother

Mary of Jerusalem

...John Mark's mother

The servant girl Rhoda scurried about her mistress's comfortably furnished bedroom, lighting Mary's three favorite lamps, plumping the pillows on her couch, jumping back to move a pomegranate to one side of the heavy cluster of purple grapes in the fruit bowl on the small bedside table — then to the windows to draw the draperies — and back to the fruit bowl to change the pomegranate again.

"Everything is just right, Rhoda," Mary smiled. "You're a good girl, and very thoughtful."

"But it's such an important night, ma'am!" Rhoda stopped abruptly and clasped her hands. "Such an important night for *you*, Mistress Mary. Just think! Your son, John Mark, is coming home — to surprise you."

Mary laughed. "Not much of a surprise once you heard he was coming, Rhoda."

"Did I do wrong to tell you?" The girl frowned.

"Not at all. If you hadn't, I'd undoubtedly have been asleep when the poor boy arrived. Now that I know, we'll be all ready for him."

231

"His room is prepared, Mistress. I've even turned down his bed."

"You are a good girl, my dear. And a good Christian, too. I'm proud of you."

"I'm glad we're known now as *Christians*," the girl beamed. "Aren't you, ma'am? Don't you love the way that name sounds?"

"Indeed I do. I'm very happy Barnabas wrote it to us. Now, it's time you went to bed, Rhoda. Good night."

The girl hesitated, curtsied, started for the door, then turned back. "Good night, ma'am, but could I say one more thing?"

"Of course."

"You meant that when you said you thought I was a good Christian, didn't you?"

"I certainly did mean it."

"Well, I just wanted you to know it's all because of you. Because you have taught me about the Lord, but mostly, I think — if I am a good Christian — it is because I live in the same house with you."

Mary smiled again, raised her two fingers in the Christian sign of recognition, and said fondly: "You and I are Christian sisters, Rhoda."

"Oh, thank you, ma'am. Good night."

"Good night."

Mary of Jerusalem looked at the closed door a long time after the girl left. I wonder if I'm so happy tonight over Rhoda's endearing loyalty to the Lord, or because my son, John Mark, is coming home again. Both, she decided, and pulled a light coverlet over her knees as she settled herself on her couch to wait for Mark. It would be wonderful having him home again, her sensitive, impetuous, active son — so like his father the last time she saw him. Mary still missed her dead husband; missed him more than ever when Mark left to travel with Paul. But what an opportunity for the boy! How blessed she

232

had been that a truly great Christian such as Paul would choose her son to help him in his important work with the new churches. She would never be able to express her thanks to God.

I wonder when John Mark will get here, she thought. Long before midnight, the messenger told Rhoda. Well, when he comes, his mother — his proud, proud mother — will be up waiting, eager to welcome him home. Mary smiled at herself, and then suddenly her smile vanished. Why was the boy coming home? When he left, it was for a much longer time than he had been gone. Was something wrong? Was he ill? She sat up, fear tightening her throat. Fear? Christians did not need to fear! The Lord had said He would be with them all — always. It was what He had said just before He ascended into heaven. The Lord was there with her. The *living* Lord. And He was with John Mark too, wherever the boy was at that moment. She smiled a little, lay back down, and tried to be thankful; determined to be patient until she heard his footsteps.

Mother and son clung to each other in silence for a long time. John Mark was strangely tense; his strong young arms squeezing the breath out of her.

Finally, she pushed him back to look at him. He forced a smile, but she was not fooled.

"Something is wrong, Mark," she said quietly. "I can tell. I am not going to insist that you talk about it, but if it will make things easier — less awkward — I already know you've come home for some painful reason. I can sense it."

The boy sat down abruptly on the foot of her couch and picked at Rhoda's grapes, his slender fingers nervous. She could see little beads of sweat on his forehead, and the night was chill.

"I — uh, I might have known you'd guess, Mother."

233

"We've never tried to deceive each other, Son."

He got up. "No, we haven't."

"You're terribly jumpy. Are you so tired? Would you rather get a good night's rest before we talk?"

"No. No, I want to talk now. I want to tell you, if I can, and then forget it."

"All right. But wouldn't it be better if you sat down?"

"I don't think so."

"Whatever you say."

"I wish you wouldn't be so — pleasant."

Mary frowned, but said nothing. Better to let the boy get to the point in his own way. She had learned that with his father long ago. Perhaps an impersonal question would help, she thought, and decided to inquire after the health of her nephew Barnabas.

"Oh, Barnabas is fine," he said. "He's — he's made for a life like that. I'm not, Mother. I — I had to get away."

"I see," Mary said carefully.

"No, you don't. You couldn't. You don't know this man Paul!"

She tried to conceal her shock, but knew she didn't. "Brother Paul? Well, I — I admit I don't know him as you who travel with him, but — "

"I *did* travel with him. Not any more." The boy sat down suddenly and looked directly at her, pleading for understanding. "Mother, he's a great man. There isn't a more devout Christian anywhere in the known world. He's a magnificent preacher. A little long-winded, perhaps, but God honors his work. You know how excited I was when we left on this first missionary journey. I thought God had given me the highest blessing a young man could be given. With my whole heart, I wanted to go. I felt God had called me to go. And while we worked on the island of Cyprus, I enjoyed it. Well, most of it. But then, conditions began to change."

"Conditions?"

234

"The people in Pamphylia, Mother; they were so crude, so ignorant, so backward in their outlook on everything! Why, we all worked as hard as we knew how to work, and I doubt that one person came to believe in the Lord. Even Brother Paul got nowhere with them. The travel was rough; the distances so long between towns; the sleeping accommodations were — well, I wouldn't even want you to know some of the places I've had to sleep. It made no sense whatever that we stay there with those dull people, and yet *he* drove us all as though we were — cattle. He wouldn't give up. When we got to the city of Perga, I knew I had made my last trip with him. Whatever Paul said, everyone obeyed. I know he's the greatest among us all, but the whole missionary journey, which was supposed to be spreading the good news of the risen Lord, turned into a retinue of servants — including me — taking orders from Brother Paul, the leader!"

Mary was quiet for several minutes. Then she asked, "Did Brother Paul still need you when you left?"

She saw the boy's shoulders slump. "I had been his personal attendant. I ran his errands, wrote his letters, took his messages over hot, dirty miles — sometimes where the roads were only cattle paths." He got up again. "Yes, he still needed me, but he didn't try to stop me from leaving."

"And why do you think he didn't, John Mark?"

"How do I know? I suppose he thought 'good riddance.'"

"Have I spoiled you, son? Did your father and I do this to you by bringing you into a world where everything was too easy for you?"

He whirled to look at her, his face dark and angry. "I knew you'd say that!"

235

Mary studied him closely, but said nothing, and suddenly she saw tears in his eyes. She reached her hand to him, and the boy fell to his knees and buried his head in her

arms as he used to do when something had gone dreadful-
ly wrong, when he was truly ashamed of himself. She
patted his head and waited.

"God forgive me," he murmured, "for blaming Brother
Paul."

"God will forgive you, son. He has already."

"I wasn't man enough, Mother," he said, his face still
hidden. "Maybe Brother Paul will forgive me someday
— and give me another chance. Help me grow up,
Mother; help me."

* * * * * * * * * *

This vignette is, of course, mainly fictionized, but it
could have happened. There are enough scattered facts
about John Mark and his mother, Mary of Jerusalem, and
Paul and Barnabas and the trouble they had on their
missionary journeys, so that when the boy deserted Paul at
Perga, something like this could well have happened.

I hope Mary has spoken for herself to us in the imagined
scene with her troubled son. I admire her almost more
than any other woman in the Bible. She was born to the
good life, or at least she married into it. Her husband
was a respected man in their community, and when he
died, evidently at a rather early age (John Mark was
young, about twenty, when he first went with Paul), he
left his widow well cared for. Still, she had the difficult
job of rearing their son alone, with no father to discipline
or counsel him.

That Mark grew up, we know. After all, he is the author
of the second gospel — one of the most perceptive and
well placed pieces of literature in the entire Bible. He
did not stay a mother's boy; he matured, and apparently
would have gone with Paul later on another journey, had
Paul agreed. Mary's son outgrew his softness, his unwill-
ingness to suffer for the cause of Christ.

I credit Mary with this. Her heart stayed open to her

236

temperamental son, just as her lovely house stayed open to the dusty feet and the sometimes disorderly conduct of the members of the early church in Jerusalem. Mary was a new Christian — they all were. But her poise, her warmth, her wisdom, her sensitivity were witness to the fact that she followed a *living* Lord. I am sure Mary *acted* most of the time as though His life was in hers — as it was. She must have been there at Pentecost. In fact, it is quite possible that Pentecost took place in the same upper room at her home. It is also probable that Jesus ate His Last Supper with His disciples in that room. After all, many believe that Mark was the young man who ran out from under his cloak in the Garden the night they arrested Jesus.

Mary saw to it that her son was constantly exposed to Christ — before His death and after His resurrection. She was an active part of the early church. She sat in no special pew, feeling aloof from those less fortunate than she. Mary had church in her house. She took the resurrection literally. To her, it was not a theory; it was a fact in history. She also took Pentecost literally. She must have been there; certainly she lived as though she had been.

John Mark had been with Paul and Barnabas in Antioch when believers in the risen Lord began to be called Christians. The boy had a firsthand chance to find out what the name meant, I believe, from his own mother.

Rufus' mother

...and Paul's

Rufus' mother

...and Paul's

In Corinth, at the close of his third missionary journey, the Apostle Paul, at the height of his powers, sat in his room in the home of Gaius, his fellow Christian, dictating to Tertius the end of a long letter to the members of the church in Rome. Every day for may days, he and his amanuensis had labored over the epistle, Paul weighing each word, eager for those who would read it to understand.

"We are almost finished, Tertius," he said, pressing his fingers against his weak, weary eyes. "But before I give you the final part of the letter, read the salutation again, will you please?"

Young Tertius turned back to the beginning of Paul's letter to the Romans and read: "To all God's beloved in Rome, who are called to be saints: Grace to you and peace from God our Father and the Lord Jesus Christ. First, I thank my God through Jesus Christ for all of you, because your faith is proclaimed in all the world. For God is my witness, whom I serve with my spirit in the gospel of his Son, that without ceasing I mention you always in my prayers, asking that somehow by God's will I may now at

241

last succeed in coming to you. For I long to see you, that I may impart to you some spiritual gift to strengthen you, that is, that we may be mutually encouraged by each other's faith, both yours and mine."

The older man held up his hand. "Enough, Tertius. Thank you. I can finish the letter now. I just had to make sure my beginning showed the warmth and love I really feel in my heart toward those Roman Christians."

Paul leaned back on his couch, closed his eyes a moment, and then said, "I must mention some of them by name in my farewell words. I have not been to Rome, but many of them I have known and worked with elsewhere — in Ephesus, in Colossae, in Corinth." He glanced at Tertius. "Rest your hand a moment longer while I recall their names. I would hate to forget even one who had been faithful, and there are many. Faithful Phoebe will be taking this letter to Rome for me. I must remember to urge them to receive her with love. And then there are my fellow workers, with whom I used to make tents, Prisca and Aquila; there is my beloved Epaenetus, my first convert to Christ in Asia; there is also Mary, and Andronicus and Junias, my kinsmen and fellow prisoners. I will want to greet Ampliatus, Urbanus, and my beloved Stachys; Apelles, and all the family of Aristobulus; another kinsman of mine, Herodion, and the family of Narcissus; Tryphaena, Tryphosa, and hard-working Persis." Paul sat up, a tender look on his face. "And I must not, oh, I must not forget to mention, with a heart full of love, beloved Rufus, so eminent in the Lord."

The apostle was silent a moment, smiling over his thoughts of Rufus.

"Brother Rufus is the son of Simon the Cyrenian, isn't 242   he, sir?" Tertius' eyes shone with wonder. "What must it be like to know that one's own father helped our Lord carry His cross that day? What must it be like, sir?"

"I've wondered about that many times, Tertius. What

comes to me when I think of it is that I have been asked to take up my own cross. Perhaps that special kind of contact has been some human incentive for Rufus to grow as he has grown in Christ. His father must have been a humble man. Rufus is indeed humble. Oh, and I must not, I could not fail to send my warmest greetings to the mother of Rufus — my mother also. My great-hearted, gentle mother in the Lord."

"You have told me many times, sir, of her kindness to you, of her service to you."

"More than mere service, Tertius. She has *shown* me Christ in her life. A simple, profound woman, with a faith that has many times strengthened my body. Rufus' mother has never been one for much public activity — her main service is to love. This she does far better than most of us."

"Do you suppose she was there — that day, Sir? Did you ever ask her if she stood nearby and *saw* her husband help our Lord carry the cross?"

"No, although I admit I've wanted to ask her. But if she felt I needed to know, she would volunteer to tell me." Paul's eyes filled with tears. "She is a real mother to me, too, as she has always been to Rufus."

* * * * * * * * * *

Could any woman be paid a greater tribute by a greater man than the Lord's apostle, Paul? In the closing lines of his letter to the members of the church in Rome, Paul does not mention her name, but he does a far more poignant thing — he calls her *his* mother.

It has always seemed to me that in not mentioning her name, he has done her even greater honor. It is as though he is saying in effect, "All of you know the mother of Rufus; there is no need to call her by name. She is dear and familiar to everyone there, I am sure, as she is to me."

When he spoke of some of the others, he commented on their special efforts, their particular standings in the Lord,

243

or in their service to Paul. For example, when he greets Prisca and Aquila, he calls them ". . . my fellow workers in Christ Jesus, who risked their necks for my life." He points out that Epaenetus was his (Paul's) first Asian convert; that Apelles "is approved in Christ." Persis has "worked hard in the Lord." But when he comes to Rufus' mother, he simply claims her as his own mother.

I have wondered, too, if she stood in the crowd along the Via Dolorosa that day. Did the very sight of His bruised and battered face open her heart forever to His love? To showing His love to those who needed it as Paul did? There is no record that Paul's own mother ever became a follower of Christ. It could well be that he was ostracized by his orthodox Jewish parents, counted as dead. At any rate, Paul needed the woman whose husband helped Jesus carry His heavy cross as He stumbled through the narrow Jerusalem streets that day — and she was there when he needed her. As her husband had been there when Jesus needed him.

She must have been a good mother to Paul. No man who has ever walked our earth has carried his own cross more courageously, while "bearing about in his own body the marks of the Lord" he followed through every hour of every day.

God has this to say to us, I believe, through the woman Paul called "mother": *Be there, my daughter. Be there when you're needed.*

BIBLIOGRAPHY

Edersheim, Alfred, *Life and Times of Jesus the Messiah* (Eerdmans)

Deen, Edith, *All the Women of the Bible* (Harper)

Deen, Edith, *Family Living in the Bible* (Harper)

Lockyer, Herbert, *The Women of the Bible* (Zondervan)

Miller, M.S. and J.L., *Harper's Bible Dictionary* (Harper)

Price, Eugenia, *Beloved World* (Zondervan)

Price, Eugenia, *Learning to Live From the Gospels* (Lippincott)

Tenney, Merrill C., *Zondervan Pictorial Bible Dictionary* (Zondervan)

Scripture quotations are from the Revised Standard Version

DISCOVERIES

DISCOVERIES

Made from Living My New Life

EUGENIA PRICE

DOUBLEDAY

New York   London   Toronto   Sydney   Auckland

A Main Street Book
PUBLISHED BY DOUBLEDAY
a division of Bantam Doubleday Dell Publishing Group, Inc.
1540 Broadway, New York, New York 10036

MAIN STREET BOOKS, DOUBLEDAY, and the portrayal of a building with a tree are
trademarks of Doubleday, a division of
Bantam Doubleday Dell Publishing Group, Inc.

Discoveries was previously published by Zondervan Publishing House in 1953.
The Main Street edition is published by arrangement with Eugenia Price.

To
Ellen Riley Urquhart
. . . the one through whom He found me

PREFACE

This little book was written forty years ago and has remained in print since. It is the very first book I ever published, although many believe that *The Burden Is Light* was the first. *Discoveries* is a random collection of short essays which, if some of the exuberant style is any indication, must have poured from a heart running over with excitement at what I was discovering in my new Christian life.

After rereading it and chuckling at some of the very "young" sounds in it, I find that most of what few changes I have made involve only sentence structure and the scooping out of handfuls of exclamation points. In those first days as a believer, everything was exclamatory. I confess that certain flat, sweeping statements have a glib ring to me now—almost amusing, as one is naturally amused at a child. You see, most of it was written during the second and third years of my new Christian life. Yet I am amazed, not only to find how much He had taught me back then in such a short time, but that my life is still centered forty eventful years later in the Person of Jesus Christ Himself. The center has not changed at all. I now see more objectively, make room for far more differing opinions about God, but I can honestly say that I remain a follower of Jesus Christ *because* I believe more strongly than ever that God the Father did reveal Himself in Jesus. It was on that point that I became a Christian; it is because God is discoverable in Jesus that I remain so.

Christians believe that God "paid a visit to this planet" in the Person of Jesus of Nazareth *so that anyone can discover His true intentions toward each one of us.* "I and the Father are one," Jesus declared. Turning from self-mastery for me was almost automatic the moment I realized that. If God is like this young Man-God who loved us enough to become one of us, I almost have no choice but to trust Him. Not easy, but certainly simple.

Forty years later, none of that has changed for me. I am still not affiliated with any particular "christian" organization and I cringe and grieve to see others who call themselves Christian build entire organizations (more political than spiritual) in order to justify sitting in judgment upon those of us who do not agree with them on every "jot and tittle." But when Christ Himself remains central, we stay in at least some kind of balance—*and* in a meeting place.

I was in my early thirties when I wrote *Discoveries*. I am in my late seventies now, and because there is no end to the wonder, I am still a discoverer.

EUGENIA PRICE
St. Simons Island, Georgia
May 1993

Contents

Discoveries

Concerning
Discipleship

1.

His
Viewpoint
or Mine?

I WAS LED INTO a personal walk with Jesus Christ by a disciple of Jesus Christ, who immediately set about fulfilling the command of her Lord, to make a disciple of me.

Jesus did not say, just before He went to sit at the right hand of the Father, "Go and save men." He said: "Go and make *disciples* of men." As I see it, a disciple is simply one who learns. One who puts himself in position to learn, and above all, one who is *willing* to learn. Does that include us? Are we in position to learn about Him? Or are we locked up, bolted down within the rigid confines of our own creed and unable to see beyond it into the breath-taking distances of God? Are we devoted to the task of bringing others into a personal relationship with Jesus Christ? Or are we bound and determined to bring them into agreement with ourselves?

Jesus said: "When the Spirit of truth comes, He will guide you into all the truth." Do we really trust the Spirit of truth or do we merely trust what *we* understand *about* Him?

Are we dogmatic *clingers* to our doctrines? Or are we *held* in the everlasting arms of Him who promised that He would never leave us nor forsake us? Are we believers in the things we know *about* Jesus Christ? Or are we believers *in* Jesus Christ Himself? Are we disciples? Are we learners? *Are* we?

What does it mean to be a disciple? Quite simply, from my own experience and from having been privileged to watch a few of God's real disciples live their daily lives, I would venture to say that if one is to become a disciple of Jesus Christ, one *must* have the *viewpoint* of Jesus Christ.

Viewpoint is a noun meaning point of view. When we look at the definition of the word "view," doors begin to open in our minds. Our "view" is widened. If we carry the definition of a disciple as one who has the viewpoint of Christ into Webster's rather complete defining of the word "view," one horizon after another collapses and we see out and away into still more of the distances of God.

First of all, "view" means the "very act of seeing." *Do we see what Christ sees in the people around us?*

Secondly, "view" means "a mental survey; a just view of the arguments." *Do we have Christ's "just view" of the arguments (rational and irrational), which we hear going on about us even among Christians?*

Thirdly, Mr. Webster says that "view" means "power of seeing; reach or range of sight." Do we have Christ's "power of seeing" those whom He sends us to help? *Do we have His "range of sight" into their needs and the causes of their separation from Him?*

Mr. Webster further defines the word "view" as "mode of looking at anything; judgment; as to state one's view of policy." Do we look through the eyes of Christ at His sheep and their predicaments? Or do we judge for ourselves as we scoff and condemn silently, the while we deceive even ourselves into believing we are leaving the judgment to Him? And the last half of that particular definition of the word "view" embraces the stating of one's view of a policy. How

Christlike are we in our view of our Christian brother's policy when it happens to disagree with our own?

"Viewpoint": a commonly used word with uncommon depths of meaning when we as believers in Jesus Christ dare to examine our own discipleship in the light of whether or not *we* live and operate from the viewpoint of the One in whom we believe.

For the next few pages we are going to go into some of the implications of having the viewpoint of Christ. Again, I confess to sharing my brand-new understanding of these things. Perhaps the reader's years of experience in walking with God will far overshadow my recent entrance into the brightness of the life for which we were born. But no matter how new the Christian follower, Jesus Christ *was* "in the beginning." And His viewpoint has and always will be without variation. For He is the rock on which our every premise may rest, and from which we may safely project our flights of understanding. If our discoveries are real and if they are true, they will return to rest upon the rock. They will be checked and re-checked and directed and patiently re-directed by the Spirit of truth who, thank God, *has* come and does dwell within us if we believe.

I believe. I have given myself over to Him. He is mine and I am His. I want to share with you what I feel He is teaching me concerning true discipleship. I want to confess my stumblings and share with you my victories and rejoice the while in the Lord, whom to know is life eternal; whom to know is to belong to and to love — forever.

2.

No
Condemnation

WE HAVE DWELT at some length on what it means to
have the viewpoint of Jesus Christ. We stated that it is impossible for a Christian to be a true disciple unless he possesses the viewpoint of Christ as his own. I have found this
to be invariably true of my own personal life. Unless we
view a dilemma in another's life as Christ views it, we are
not able to help that person to a lasting solution of the
problem. Unless we face the problems that arise in our life
from the viewpoint of the One who has redeemed us, we
do not find their workable solutions.

But even more important than seeing *problems* from the
viewpoint of Christ is the absolute necessity of looking at
other *people* — whether believers or non-believers — as Jesus
Christ looks at them. To do this, *we* must stay out of the
picture completely. With mere *human* perception, no matter
how educated or how keen that perception, we simply *cannot*
see others as Jesus Christ sees them. We see them smudged
by our own shortcomings. We see them cracked and splin-
tered around the edges because too often we look from the
viewpoint of self-justification, especially if we happen not to

have been burdened with one of the particular faults or sins under which our neighbors labor. We see them bent and shapeless because they happen to have fallen into a particular pit which, by the grace of God, we passed over.

Or, we see them as strangers, out of our world, beyond our comprehension; and therefore well-nigh impossible to help, because we have not shared in their specific trouble or sin. For example, if we have not drunk excessively or at all, we look in wide-eyed amazement at the alcoholic who simply will not drop the bottle even when he or she sees the damage the bottle is causing.

We, being human, will distort our fellow men through our own spiritual eyes, unless and until we have the viewpoint of Christ. And we can only have this at last, by a complete and entire surrender of our selves (including our precious viewpoints) into the hands of the living God. Christ, alone, through His Holy Spirit, can give us the viewpoint which He has.

We believe the viewpoint of Christ must begin at the Cross of Christ. We cannot look at our fellow human beings with the viewpoint of Christ unless we can see them as He saw them — from the Cross. And the viewpoint of the Christ of the Cross is summed up in His own words spoken from that wrack of torture: "Father, *forgive* them, for they know not what they do."

The viewpoint of Christ, then, must be one of *no condemnation;* because a viewpoint of condemnation implies only one thing — self-righteousness within the heart of the one who condemns. And self-righteousness within the believer implies only one thing — the viewpoint of the *believer,* rather than the viewpoint of the One in whom he believes.

The circle is vicious and subtle.

But let us look at the pattern of the earthly life of our Lord for a moment. He was born in the lowest place a man can be born. I believe the Father picked out a stable for His Son's birthplace so no human being in all the ages after could say, "My background isn't good enough for me to become a Christian." No one . . . *no one* can be born in more meager surroundings than was our Lord.

From the point of view of His birth and the conditions surrounding it, can we condemn anyone among our fellow men no matter what their beginnings?

Or, let us look at the baptism of Jesus of Nazareth. "Then cometh Jesus from Galilee to Jordan unto John, to be baptized by him." To be baptized by John the Baptist, the people stood in line along the bank of the Jordan River. Can you picture Him, "The Lamb of God who taketh away the sin of the world," standing there patiently in line between a repentant thief and a woman of the streets, waiting His turn to be baptized with the others? We can picture Him doing nothing else. For He came to serve, not to be served. To save, not to condemn.

I testify from my own experience that if the one whom God used to lead me into a personal relationship with Jesus Christ had in any way, by the merest shadow of inference, chanced to condemn me during those first tense days as the Holy Spirit worked within my heart, I would not be writing these lines now. I know now how difficult it was for her. It is not easy for one who loves Jesus above all else to sit and hear His name blasphemed and used carelessly to punctuate casual conversation. It is not easy to have one's reason for living ridiculed. It is not easy to *be* ridiculed for Christ's sake.

But neither was it easy for Him to hang there hearing His own blood drain from His pain-twisted body and pray for the forgiveness of those who crucified Him. It did not take the usual dozen men to hold Jesus as they laid Him flat on the rude cross beam of the Cross. He lay there offering no resistance, making no move in self-defense as the blunt nails were driven into His outstretched hands and feet.

When the Cross was lifted up and dropped into the excavation in the ground, He made no cry of protest. He *prayed* for forgiveness for those who lifted Him up! *In this viewpoint of Christ from the Cross is the open secret of the victorious life of discipleship available to you and to me.*

If we are to have the viewpoint of Christ we cannot condemn, we can only *care.*

3.

No
Hopeless
Cases

WHEN ONE TRUE DISCIPLE of Jesus Christ thought on the vast, unending resources of the One whom he followed, he wrote: ". . . him that is able to do exceeding abundantly above all that we ask or think, according to the power that worketh in us."

The disciple, of course, was St. Paul. One who had, beyond the shadow of a doubt, the viewpoint of Jesus Christ. And, because he had this viewpoint, Paul knew for a fact that if *he* stayed sufficiently out of the way, the Holy Spirit of God could and would do *through* him (Paul) "exceeding abundantly above all that we ask or think."

Do we as followers of Jesus Christ really *believe* this? We say we believe the Bible to be the holy inspired Word of God. We say we believe the Pauline epistles, but do we actually believe that Jesus Christ *can* do exceedingly abundantly above all that we ask or think? If we do, then why don't we act like it by acting *on* that promise?

Do we or do we not believe that there are any *hopeless cases* where Jesus Christ is concerned? I am constrained to repeat that question — not for our sakes, but for His sake:

Do we or do we not believe that there are any hopeless cases where Jesus Christ is concerned?
What about the alcoholic or the inveterate liar or the gambler or the prostitute over whose darkened, frenzied, anxious lives have passed year after year of despair and failure? What about these people? As I write these lines I am half-listening for my telephone to ring, hoping against hope that a warm-hearted, gentle-mannered but seemingly hopeless alcoholic will call from somewhere in the cold, rainy shadows of this night along Chicago's Skid Row. I am trusting God that this boy will at last begin to *act* upon the knowledge he already possesses about his own "hopeless" case. This boy has known for ten years what he must do. He knows he must surrender one last thing to Christ. My friend and I have been praying and trying again with him for more than two years. His Christian mother in Little Rock, Arkansas, prays with us and believes with us that even though the years are piling up over her son's head, there is no such thing as a hopeless case with Jesus Christ.
There are no hopeless cases in Christ. If we believe there are, we are looking at the *sin* in the so-called hopeless case, or at the *sinner.* We simply are not looking at Christ and His resources. There are no hopeless cases with "him that is able to do exceeding abundantly above all that we ask or think."
A Christian believer shook my hand after a speaking engagement not long ago and wonderingly shook her head too as she asked: "How do you dare stand up there and promise that there are no hopeless cases when you've only been a Christian for such a short time? My brother-in-law's been a gambler for twenty years. We've never stopped praying that God would change him. But he's still at it. And we've just decided he's a hopeless case!"
I can stand anywhere and promise anyone that there are no hopeless cases in Christ on the full authority of the Son

Himself who said: "I am come that they might have life, and that they might have it more abundantly."

I can promise that in Him there are no hopeless cases because my Lord dared say of Himself what no mere human being ever dared say: "I am the way, the truth, and the life." And He did not mean a way of darkness and despair and sin and self-imprisonment. He meant the way of freedom and hope and eternal life. He meant the way *out* of darkness into the light of His love. And if Jesus Christ cannot back up the startling statements He made, if He cannot back up the claims He made, then He is the biggest phony who ever walked the face of this earth! If I cannot believe Him, whom can I believe?

More than that, even more than being able to put my whole weight down upon the promise of Christ, upon the spoken word of Christ, I can promise anyone, any time, anywhere that in Him are no hopeless cases because He was able to redeem *me!*

Quite quietly and quite calmly I stake my eternal life on the *fact* of my Saviour and my Lord, Jesus Christ. I know that when He looked down at me three and a half years ago, He did not see a hopeless case at all. He saw another creation of His, twisted all out of His plan and His nature by sin and self-will and hardness of heart. He saw one of His creations turned almost completely backwards to what He had intended her to be. But He did not see a hopeless case at all. Because He knew *Himself.* He saw *me* from the viewpoint of Himself. And He knew His own resources.

The true disciple *must* have the viewpoint of his Lord. And Jesus Christ knows that for Him, there are *no* hopeless cases.

4.

Innocence
Is Not
Purity

IT MAY SEEM a presumptuous thing to do to begin a meditation by disagreeing point blank with Mr. Webster. And, I do not disagree in a general sense. But where two words in particular are concerned, I must disagree from the standpoint of their spiritual meaning to a true disciple of Christ.

Webster contends that they are practically synonymous. In two sections of his definition, he uses them interchangeably. Spiritually this is impossible. And yet many Christians not only use them interchangeably, to their own confusion of soul, but they also *act* upon them interchangeably, which results in the department of utter confusion for new Christians and non-believers.

What are these two words? They are: "innocence" and "purity."

Spiritually, I contend, they are not the same. And I have experienced in my own life, the confusion and heartache and inner damage which result from well-meaning Christians acting as though they *were* one and the same.

Isn't *innocence* the state in which babies are born? And

isn't *purity* an outright gift of God? Are we not *made pure,* because of what Jesus did for us on the Cross, only *after* we have been *born again* into that purity which comes from Him? And *only* from Him?

We are *born innocent* at our physical birth. But we are *made pure* by faith in Jesus Christ. And faith in Him means we dare to follow Him. "Surely he hath borne our griefs, and carried our sorrows: yet we did esteem him stricken, smitten of God, and afflicted. *But he was wounded for our transgressions,* he was bruised for our *iniquities;* the chastisement of our peace was upon him; and with his stripes we are healed. [Because] *all* we like sheep *have gone astray;* we have turned *every one to his own way;* and the Lord hath laid on *him* the iniquity of us *all."*

"With *his* stripes we are healed" — *made pure.* We were *born* physically in *innocence.* We are *made pure* by Christ.

"Well," you say, "I believe all that. I do not contend that I was born pure. I am a true believer in the redemption of Jesus Christ. I know that includes me as just another sheep who went astray. I know I can claim no purity outside that which Christ has given me. I know I have been *made pure.*

All right, if we know that, then why is it that some of us do not behave as though we know it? Until she saw the true spiritual meanings of *purity* and *innocence* a well-meaning mother confused the issues in her family and in her own life by assuming that her innocence of certain sins of which her family was guilty somehow made *her* pure. She would shake her head prettily and say: "My goodness, I just don't see how they can drink that old stuff!" Or, "How can you swear every other breath like that?" Or "I never *wanted* to do those things!"

Sound familiar? Do you know someone like that? And does his very attitude seem to condemn you? Does this person's insistence that he has never even been tempted along *your* "disgusting lines" make you want either to bop him on his self-righteous head or run and hide your own head and give up trying to find Christ's answer to your own trouble? I know this is not a far-fetched reaction because I have had it myself. I have watched others smart under it. I have heard Christian young people sneer and act superior with their fellow students who drink. Thus they imply, if they do not say, "*I* just don't see *how* they can do it! *How* can they cheapen themselves?" The fellow students smart under their criticism and go on running from Christ.

Now, please do not misunderstand. Having lived in the world of paganism for almost eighteen years, I am the first to be glad and thankful when a Christian boy or girl grows all the way to maturity without sampling the world's interests. *But* I plead that they do just that — *grow all the way to maturity!* For Jesus' sake and for their own sakes. And for the sake of those whom they shut out of the kingdom by their own confusion of the spiritual meanings of the two words, "innocence" and "purity." I contend that innocence in an adult approaches stupidity. Again, do not misunderstand my meaning here. I do not advocate that anyone try the world in order to be delivered directly from worldly sins into the state of purity given only by Christ. He was without sin, and yet He reached down as far as is necessary to lift up the lowest sinner. He did not curl His lip and assume a lofty attitude and flaunt His innocence by reminding the populace that He "had never been interested in those things!"

I have tried my share and more of the pleasures of the world. And yet there are things I have never tried, simply because they did not interest me. But, do I have a right to curl my lip at those who *have* fallen on those points? Does my *innocence* of their particular sin give me a sense of purity on that point? If I think it does, God forgive me. I am not allowing Jesus Christ to live through me if this is so. Jesus was *pure* — not pompously innocent. And I am pure because He has *made* me pure.

Perhaps you have never loved the taste of whiskey. Perhaps you have never stolen anything. Perhaps you have never broken up a home. *But,* have you never shaded the truth in a conversation? Have you never told a white lie? Have you never lost your temper? Have you never criticized a fellow human being? Have you never been quick to fly to your own defense? Have you never been jealous? Have you never felt sorry for yourself? Are these not sins? Are they not transgressions for which He was wounded? Is anyone alive completely innocent of all these sins of the disposition? No. No one. But we can be made *pure*, thanks be to Him who "increased in wisdom and in stature"; who grew up into the maturity of deep sympathy and understanding of the failures of men; who not only expects us to do the same, but who daily offers us His grace and strength that we might be able to do it.

5.

His Purpose
for
Other People

IN MY OWN LIFE, I have found that if I am truly following Christ, as a disciple follows his master, I do not have to concern myself about — myself. I do not have to wonder whether or not I will be at the right place at the right time in order to accomplish a certain end. I do not have to pick my friends. I do not need, even as a Christian, to hand out solutions to others in need. I do not need to do anything but obey the One whom I profess to trust enough to follow.

It is not easy for a convinced follower of Christ to keep silent many times when the answer to another's problem seems so evident. But there are times when the problems and sorrows of humanity are too terrible for words. And sympathetic silence, deep with the presence of Christ, performs its own miracles. We must be able to express our faith in words, but actions speak louder than words every time. We must not be disturbed if we do not always *have* the answer. But every minute of our lives we must *be* the answer.

We do not need to *have* the answer, but we do need to *be* the answer.

This is simply said, but not simply done. Coming completely into the viewpoint of Jesus Christ is painful, because it means the dying out of our points of view. But it also means the birth in us of *His* point of view, and that is added pain, since birth is usually more painful than death.

We must decide whether or not we are willing to "fill up that which is behind of the afflictions of Christ." Either we are willing or we are not willing. Only we can decide.

But if *you* decide within your own heart that you want to "walk in the light as he is in the light," in close discipleship with the Master, on an intimate, friendship basis, then there is still another aspect of His viewpoint which you must take for your own: *You must completely identify yourself with His purpose for other people.*

The real meaning of this is not apparent at first. At least the apparent meaning is far from the entire meaning. At first glance we would think this means that since He said, "Go ye into all the world and make disciples," our efforts toward bringing others into the Christian life would constitute "identifying ourselves with His purpose for other people."

This is true. But it is only part of the deepest meaning of complete identification with His intent in the individual lives of those with whom we come in contact. We simply cannot help winning *some* if we ourselves are in complete contact with Christ. We cannot be in contact with Him, unless He indwells us and lives again on this earth in our bodies. And since He Himself said: "I, if I be lifted up . . . will draw all men unto me," we will, if His words are true, win *some*. Those of us who love Him and rejoice in the fulness of the wonder of the life hid with Christ in God find it difficult to keep still about this enchanted life. We don't witness because we believe it is expected of us. We simply do it because we can't help it. And so, winning others, as essential as it is, comes as a fruit of belonging entirely. And we, who mean to go all the way with Him, must delve deeper and find still other ways of identifying ourselves with His purpose in our lives.

In my experience with this deeper delving, I have stumbled and blundered most noticeably at the times when I felt perfectly justified in using my *common sense*. I do not believe we can repeat too often the dust-raising truth that *if common sense had been enough, Jesus Christ would not have needed to die!*

Let me illustrate by a personal experience. Sometime ago after a broadcast I was asked to talk to a brilliant actor, who had struggled vainly with the bottle for years. Now, normally the opportunity to talk with anyone from my old world B.C. is one of the dear delights of my heart, but this particular request seemed to offer a few serious complications. I hesitated because a travel schedule had given me only four hours sleep the night before, the broadcast was an unusually difficult one to direct, *and* I was scheduled to leave town a bit after dawn the next morning for three speaking engagements in two different cities in one day.

I have long since learned that mere physical fatigue need not stop Christ's work for long. If we stay attached to the *vine*, we are constantly in line to receive the *continuous* flow of living water. And so, trying His strength has turned into an exciting experience. I was not worried about *feeling* tired. But I did hesitate momentarily for this reason: What about the three congregations of people waiting to hear me the next day? Was I being fair to drag in a tired, limp excuse for a speaker when so *many* people were involved? Common sense would have said: "Consider the previously made engagements. This actor lives in Chicago. You can talk to him when you come back. You know it will be well after midnight before you get to bed if you get involved in a conversation of that type."

Common sense said that. But I asked Jesus what His purpose in this actor's life was — for that night. I got no answer at once. But after about ten minutes in the silence with the One in whose will I want to live every minute, I had my answer. And after our conversation that night, driving home alone, my friend, the actor, stopped his car, put his head down on the steering wheel and received Jesus as his Saviour and his Lord. Having been very much aware of Christ's complete mastership of my every action and thought that night, I had talked at length about that aspect of the Christian life. So when my friend stepped "in," he knew it meant turning his back on himself — *completely.* The fact that Jesus *mastered* me intrigued him. He came in *all* the way. Jesus does not always figure in numbers. And we cannot "figure" His purpose from our viewpoint. We must do our looking and our acting — *every* minute of every hour of every day — from the viewpoint of Christ.

6.

Self-realization
vs.
Self-expenditure (I)

THERE IS SOMETHING definitely attractive in the schools of "new thought" and the cults of self-development. Much of their positive thinking could make more victorious Christians of the true followers of the divine Son of God, Jesus of Nazareth, whom the cultists merely admire as a great man. After all, Jesus Himself said, "*Let* not your heart be troubled." That requires some positive affirming on our part. (However, it is a mystery to me how an unregenerate person, a mere imitator of Christ, *could* simply ignore the pieces and let not his heart be troubled if that heart found itself in a shattered state.) There is something attractive about the self-development cults. In fact, it is so attractive that they are drawing off bored, tired, nominal Christians into their ranks every day.

And what is this attraction? The bane of the Christian's existence! *Self.* But to the man outside of Christ, the most important person in the world is *himself.* And when a religion (such as Hinduism) or a new thought school (such as the various scientific pseudo-Christian movements) encourages a man to "bring out the best within" and "develop" that all important person — himself, naturally he is going to summon his fellow man and follow after the group that tells him he's going to be just fine when he gets the best in him all shined up and declared righteous by — himself.

I repeat that reborn Christians could take some pointers here. Once we have dumped our own sinful selves into the hands of Jesus Christ our Redeemer, *then* we can expect the very best from those redeemed selves. If we cannot, in fact, if we *do* not, we underestimate our Redeemer. I believe that a "new creature," by the power of the indwelling Holy Spirit, *can* "let not" his heart be troubled. He is *enabled* to do it. He is not doing it under his own human steam; he is *enabled* to do it by Christ's indwelling presence.

None of this is new to the thoughtful disciple of Christ. But it is needed to preface what we must consider together now, as we move toward the end of our thinking on some of the characteristics of the true disciple of Jesus Christ. Here is the focal point: We must shift our perspective from *self-realization* to *self-expenditure.*

If we are to be disciples, we must have the viewpoint of Christ, and in order to have His viewpoint, we must stop trying to *realize* our *selves,* and begin *spending ourselves* for Him. Back in my B.C. days, I was an accomplished spendthrift. Now, the Lord has taken that sin, turned it inside out, redeemed it, but is still *fulfilling* that desire to spend by allowing me the unspeakable joy and stimulus of *spending myself for Him.* I have found Jesus Christ to be the kind of God who never asks us to give up a single thing which He does not replace with "good measure pressed down . . . and running over." When my dear friend, Ellen, led me into the presence of the One who transformed my life, she needed at the last moment to urge me only to this extent: "Give Him all of your life, and He will hurl all of His life back into its place."

Could I resist an exchange like that? No, I could not.

Thank God, I did not. And although the deep-down excitement that flooded my very being that day, October 2, 1949, when this eternal transaction was made, has ebbed and flowed at times, not once have I lost sight of the fact that in the terms of that eternal transaction, *I* had promised to give Him *all of my* life. I became aware also that the transaction was continuous as well as instantaneous. As with all of us, at times I have jerked myself back from His hands, and have started "throwing cues" according to what I considered good timing. But at no time in my entire life have I known heart misery to equal my own when I have done this — even for a few minutes. And so, my soul vibrates with joy that I have been made aware that if I continue to give to Him, He continues to give to me — good measure, pressed down, and shaken together, and running over.

And when I speak of spending myself, I do not mean the long tiring trips and loss of sleep entailed by a top-heavy speaking schedule. I do not mean the nights spent in pounding the typewriter in order to meet script and book deadlines. These could easily fall into the category of *self-realization* — *if* my conception of self-expenditure ended there.

But, as a disciple of Jesus Christ, I believe that we have no right to be anything but doormats to every human being who does not know the *full measure* of joy we know in belonging to Jesus personally. And the statement should be examined closely, because it implies much more than it states. Every human being who does not know the full measure of joy might seem to mean every *non-believer*. But it means much more than that. I feel ashamed if for His sake, I am at times unwilling to be or careless about being "broken bread and poured out wine" for all Christians who have *not* found the *fullness* of the life hid with Christ in God. I have wept into my pillow many nights because of the multitudes of unhappy, unvictorious, worried, anxious Christians with whom I have spoken here and there. And because I have finally yielded my own stubborn (converted) self into the hands of Him who surrendered His life for *me,* I can only be "broken bread and poured out wine" until these anxious Christians as well as the non-believers with whom I come in contact are brought into the fullness of the life hid with Christ in God.

If we are trying to realize the best in ourselves and save our energies for our own troubles, we do not have the viewpoint of Jesus Christ. We are *saving* ourselves in the face of what He did to save us *from* ourselves. We are saving ourselves when, for love of Him, we should be *spending* ourselves.

7.

Self-realization
vs.
Self-expenditure (II)

(I COULD FILL THE PAGES of an entire book with what I have discovered about the miracles that result in a redeemed human life when the will is fully surrendered to Jesus Christ. A fully surrendered will and a completely yielded life mean a life of true discipleship, with fruit hanging from every thriving branch. Christ allows the fruit to grow on the branches while He, the Vine, quietly and lovingly supports and feeds each branch with His own life).

We continue thinking together in this *essential* characteristic of the true disciple: *self-expenditure* in place of self-realization.

We resign as masters of the universe and allow Christ to take over at conversion. But, just as the same basic law of nature that brings the bud to the apple tree for the first time continues operative between the Creator and the apple tree for the duration of the tree's life, so the same divine law that brings about our spiritual rebirth remains operative between the disciple and the Creator forever.

In the deepest sense, perhaps we could say He *creates*

discipleship in us. Our part is to let Him do it. No human being alive *prefers* in his own raw, human nature, to deny himself for others. No human being *prefers* to lose his life in order to save it. He prefers to save his life and take his chances on finding still more. This is not observation culled from tomes on the psychology of human nature. This is fact from my own life B.C. Until Jesus Christ reached down and took me to Himself, my philosophy of life (if such I had in fact) ran something like this: "Get all I can get for myself today and then take my chances on being able to get even more tomorrow!"

This did not make me an unpleasant, greedy creature. This simply made me resemble people. I was generous and kind to those about whom I cared, or who pleased me for one reason or another; but I would not give one iota of myself for someone about whom I did not care. I was the most important person in the world to me. Period.

I probably would not have admitted it then, because indeed, in all honesty, I simply did not see myself that way. How could I? That is looking at human nature through the clear eyes of Christ. He sees anything that comes between Himself and His creatures for whom He died, as sin. And the self in that creation is the root of *all* that comes between. My overdose of self blinded me *to* myself.

With these stinging truths in mind, examine your Christian life with me — right now, as I examine mine under the light of Him who *is* light. Is your cup running over? Is mine? If they are not, they should be. Jesus has plenty of living water, and if our cups are only half full it must mean they are simply not clean enough for Him to fill. He will not, He *cannot* pour His living water into a dirty cup.

Now, we can soil our cups and pitchers in many ways. Worry, fear, anxiety, stubbornness, jealousy, bitterness, resentment, temper, a critical nature, a sharp tongue — any or all of these and more can so smudge our lives that the living water, because of God's own holy nature, cannot be poured into them.

But the most frequent cause of smudge among Christians which I have found is this: *The seemingly unthinking way in which we continue to live our own lives.* When I say "unthinking," I mean that it is almost as though many are innocent of the fact that they are continuing to live their own lives. We attend our churches, work among the church groups, serve on committees, teach classes, tithe, give religious books to non-believers, intercede in prayer, keep our moral lives above reproach — and yet, we are living self-lives. Our families and our homes and our offices and our church *activities* are in the center of our lives. All for the glory of God, of course, we strive to do a better job than the other fellow did. Our churches are filled with well-meaning, hard-working, respectable Christian men and women who have their Christian *selves* in the center of their lives and *not* the person of Jesus Christ.

Jesus Christ's *person* was magnetic and powerful enough literally to *pull* me out of a life of paganism and draw me to Himself. Perhaps it is *simpler* (not easier, but *simpler*) for me to keep Him in the center of my life. After having steamed through thirty-three years under a full head of self-realization, I can do nothing now but shift completely to the viewpoint of the One who gentled my striving sinful spirit and restored me to the freedom and fulfillment He meant me to have "in the beginning."

You may spend more nights a week on church work than you spend with your family. But what would be your reaction if an alcoholic called you on the telephone at 3:30 A.M. and began mumbling and mouthing at you about the tough way life treats him? I may write half the night and speak four times the next day, but how much of the spirit of Christ will I show when, at the close of the last speaking date that next day (when my eye-lids are being propped open by the grace of God), some well-rested Christian brother comes up to me and says, "I'm glad God is no respecter of persons and that he saved you, Miss Price, but I'm sorry you had to sink so low first. And another thing, Miss Price, on your radio program seven weeks ago you said that 'whosoever believeth *in* him should not perish,' and it should have been 'whosoever believeth *on* him!' " Will I smile at that well-meaning brother and offer him my hand, mindful of the nail prints in the hand of the One who *was* no respecter of persons (thank God!) when He did reach down to save me? Will I view life from the perspective of my own touchy self, or have I truly shifted my perspective from self-realization, from self-protection, to self-*expenditure?*

What of the Christians who have never invited a non-believer to their homes for dinner? Who refuse to entertain a new, stumbling Christian because that new Christian still smokes or drinks? Who keep themselves so busy with breaking fancy cakes and pouring countless cups of coffee for the sake of "Christian fellowship" that they have no time left to be "broken bread and poured out wine" for the sake of bringing some desperate man or woman into the fellowship of Christ?

We cannot condemn our Christian brothers when we face these facts. I must confess I did at first, so stunned was I to see how complacently the average Christian moves through his respectable and protected life, literally ignoring those outside the walls of his own particular doctrinal belief. Having been "out there" and left alone by Christians for so long, my heart broke for Jesus' sake; and at first I condemned in my heart. Now, my heart still breaks for Jesus' sake, but my condemnation has turned, by His grace, to intercession for those comfortable Christian brothers and sisters who have not found the fullness and the joy of complete self-*expenditure* for the One who "is not willing that *any* should perish."

Discoveries

Concerning My
Reason for Living

8.

To Me to Live
Is Not to
Be Religious

OPENING ANOTHER LINE of discovery together, let us ask ourselves this question: Can I honestly and without reservation say, "To me to live is *Christ*"?

As disciples, *if* we are true disciples, this must be entirely a reality with us. And since we can delude ourselves and fool our friends quite innocently on this point, I feel we must give it careful scrutiny. Just what exactly does it mean? What does it mean to you when you read or repeat, "To me to live is Christ"? What does it *do* to you? Does it ring any bells? Does it cause your heart to race with joy? Does it make you want to look up, just for the sake of knowing that you can look up and see no shadow between you and this Christ?

Or is it just another Scripture text?

If it is that, repeating the words or reading them from the Bible will do no more than stir up that respect which we hold for the written-down revelation of God which we have between the covers of the greatest Book.

Or, perhaps it arouses no more than admiration within

you for the childlike humility of St. Paul, who allowed himself to be changed from a Christ-hater to one who could say without reservation that for him to live was Christ.

This altogether startling phrase could and does bring about many reactions ranging from utter perplexity in the non-believer to the quiet ecstacy of the saint whose lips form the words with the joy and certainty that add up to "foolishness to the natural man."

We pass by these varied reactions now, however, to look at the ways in which sincere, well-meaning, devoted Christians can *un*consciously misinterpret it or rephrase it. Saint Paul said: "To me to live is Christ." But how easy is it for us to say: "To me to live is to be *religious!*"

Does *this* interpretation of the immortal words ring any bells with you? With me, I am afraid if it rang anything it would be a buzzer. I do not even like the sound of the word "religious." I like it even less than I did before I surrendered my life to Christ. There are many religions. Basically they are all attempts to bridge the gap between God and man. But in only one of them, the Gospel of Christ, does God reach down for man. In the others, man reaches vainly, pathetically, anxiously toward God. And so to me, living the Christian life is not "being religious," it is belonging to a *Person* who has reached down for me. And yet, according to the lack of vitality, the lack of dynamic, the frigidity of many so-called Christian lives, this text *must* be one of the most misinterpreted texts in the entire Bible. If I say, "To me to live is to be religious," I am missing the mark entirely.

I am not only missing the mark the Lord expects me to hit, I am putting emphasis entirely in the wrong place. For example, if we say, "To me to live is to be religious," how quickly we can tread respectably and stiffly into formalism. If we say, "To me to live is to be religious," how swiftly we will mount our pedestals and attempt to serve those beneath us, without once bending our necks to look at their agony of soul and mind and body. If we say, "To me to live is to be religious," how *unlike* our Lord we will become.

For can we be like Him if we are garbed in our religious regalia high atop our pious pedestals? From that vantage point can we show the world the brotherly love of the One who stood in line with sinners to wait His turn to be baptized? Can we show the world the gentle heart of the One who always took time to heal a blind beggar and take notice of a widow's mite? Can we show the world the almighty meekness of the One who turned His blood-filled eyes to the Father to ask forgiveness for those who caused Him to shed that blood drop by precious drop? Can we, sitting on our religious pedestals, convince the world that *we* know He hung there for our sakes too? Can we show forth from a pedestal the nature of the One who was born so low no sinner could possibly claim a more lowly beginning? Can we sit on a religious pinnacle and convince anyone that we follow a Lord who was purposely born in a stable? Can we proclaim from atop our pious perches that we *serve* the One who *wants* to wash the feet of the world *through* us?

After having lived in darkness, I am much aware of the freedom and satisfaction of having the world know there is no stain or shadow in my life now; that I am forgiven by and restored to my Father. But if I say, "To me to live is to be religious or respectable or respected," I am putting the blessings of my new life in the center and not the Blesser. If I am impressed with my new purity, can I expect Jesus to be able to reach down *through* me and lift up a bitter atheist who quite naturally hates my purity? Only when I see my own holiness as His holiness poured *into* my life, only when I see my adequate life as a result of having emptied my life of my *self* and of having that empty space filled with His victorious Spirit, then and only then can His love flow through me to those in need, to those whom He needs as they need Him. To me to live is *not* to be religious. To me to live is — Christ.

Is it true with you? It can be before you turn this page.

9.

To Me to Live
Is Not to
Serve Humanity

THERE ARE MANY, too many words which are consciously or unconsciously substituted for the name of Christ in the penetrating phrase of Paul: "To me to live is Christ."

We have already looked at some length into the dangers of living as though the phrase read, "To me to live is to be *religious.*" Now let us face another substitution which is so often made in this verse in place of His wonderful name. Do not many thousands of well-meaning Christians revise the phrase to read this way: "To me to live is to serve *humanity*"?

Now, on this point, I want to be clearly understood. As a new Christian, I am daily surprised and sometimes shocked at the seeming indifference to the sufferings of humanity shown by many of those who make the most effusive Christian professions. Jesus did not say we had to believe in His atonement; He simply died and made it a reality for us when we take it by faith. He did not demand that we believe in His resurrection; He simply — arose! He does not demand that we believe in His coming again; He will simply return one day in His time. In fact, Jesus did not demand that we believe very many things on a list. But He did command that we love one another. He asked us to love God with our whole being and to love our neighbors as we love ourselves.

If we remember that on our own we are the most important persons in the world to ourselves, that last is quite an order. Literally, of course, it does not only mean the person who lives next door or even in our neighborhood. It means every human being on earth. I do not believe it means that we can respond emotionally in a positive way to every creature, but it surely does mean that we must be as *concerned* for the welfare of others as we are for ourselves. And *that* is a big order. Do we fly to the defense of others as quickly as we fly to the defense of ourselves?

No comment.

Do we pity members of the church down the street or of the opposition political party when failure strikes them as we pity our precious selves?

No comment.

Why? Because we do not love and want to serve our fellow man as we love and want to serve ourselves or those to whom we happen to react favorably.

Daily I have to spend time before the humble Christ, who asked me to love *everyone,* to allow Him to touch and transform the tender, sore spots of self-esteem and snobbery still showing up in me. It hurts to have them touched. It makes me reel and tremble for the moment to see Him changing — actually changing one of my old precious opinions of a certain person into His opinion of that person. It knocks crutch after crutch out from under my swaying ego. But when the operation is done, how relieved I am not to have to be upset or irritated the next time that particular kind of person enters my life. How safe I feel then not to need that crutch any longer to prop up my self-esteem.

Much of the barb throwing, however, between the conservatives and the liberals of Christendom, has resulted from this very point of serving humanity. The liberals tend to rephrase Paul this way: "To me to live is to serve humanity!" One such liberal friend of mine made a pithy statement to me not long ago. She contends that the liberals need to love the Lord more and the fundamentalists need to love the people more. I agree.

A social gospel alone, where the needs of humanity are placed uppermost, is but a half-gospel. But those of us who believe in a complete Gospel *must*, for the sake of Christ, learn to love the *whole man — not just his soul*. Just as we must also want to *save his soul* and not merely his body and his mind.

It is easy, exceedingly easy, to become eccentric in our sincere efforts to be true disciples of Christ. And if the emphasis is put upon any one corner of the life, it tips. So, just as "To me to live is to be religious" is off center, so is "To me to live is to serve humanity" off-center. *Eccentric.*

Thousands upon thousands of men and women all over the world spend their lives pouring themselves out for humanity. This is the highest human level of life. Truly, no one could deny that this is the highest *natural* life. But, the true disciple of the divine Jesus Christ, God incarnate, does not need to be tied to the earth by even this highest *human* or *natural* achievement. Only the twice-born Christian has access to the *super*-human and the *super*-natural, by the power of the indwelling Holy Spirit. We are insured against heart-break this way. Since the Person of the Holy Spirit is one with God the Father and with Jesus Christ, He will not "let Himself down" as He lives His life through us. Humanity will turn its back on a man. Divinity through Jesus Christ will turn the man into His own image. Humanity will break a man's heart; divinity, through Jesus Christ, will *mend* that heart.

Serving humanity is a noble aim. But it is only one of the inevitable fruits of the life of the man or woman whose every thought and word and deed shout to the world:

"To me to live is Christ!"

10.

To Me to Live Is Not to Serve Christ

We will speak elsewhere in this book about the startling fact (to some) that Jesus Christ does not want our *talents*, He wants *us*. Of course, He wants our talents too, but not *without all* the rest of us thrown in. With this in mind, and with our minds wide open, let us look still more deeply into a popular rephrasing of the all-inclusive statement of St. Paul: "To me to live is Christ."

We have thought together so far upon these rephrasings of Paul's profound declaration: "To me to live is to be *religious*"; then, "To me to live is to serve *humanity*." Now we go even deeper than these two convenient interpretations. We look honestly at an interpretation of the immortal words which would at first glance seem to be synonymous with what Paul was actually saying. Consider this with me: "To me to live is to *serve* Christ."

"To me to live is to serve Christ." "To me to live is Christ." Did not this Christ say, "Go ye into all the world and make disciples"? Did not this same Christ say, "The fields are white to harvest"? Yes, He did. And so, we must lift many of the top layers off the familiar testimony of Paul in order to reach the place at the heart of his statement which shows us the grave difference between a simple *belonging* to Christ and merely *serving* Him.

For reasons known only to Him, the Master put me almost immediately into the thick of the harvest field. One year and one week after my conversion to Jesus Christ, I stood in the control room of a large radio station directing the only "big time" Christian dramatic program about lives which had been transformed as mine had been transformed by the touch of the Holy Spirit of God. The program was well named — "Unshackled." Every fiber of its writer-producer's being vibrated with the consciousness that she, too, had been "unshackled," just as surely and from just as defeated a life as any man or woman who reached the black alleys and the dusty gutters of Chicago's Skid Row. The mail count climbed, the studio audience increased, magazine writers began to call for interviews and the requests for speaking dates poured in — more each month, until there were not enough days in the week to fill them and still continue writing "Unshackled." People clasped my hand and from sincere hearts said: "Oh, how wonderfully the Lord is using you! How glorious is your great *service* for Christ!"

And my eyes filled with tears of wonder along with theirs as I moved through the glowing days with the amazement of a child suddenly set down in a toy shop a hundred miles square. Offers came for more radio programs, for T.V. programs, for magazine articles, for columns. And instead of feeding my previously over-sized vanity, by His grace the opposite took place. I began to understand what Paul meant when he said: "I determined not to know anything among you, save Jesus Christ, and him crucified."

The Crucified Himself overshadowed me *and* my new Christian service. I became more and more drawn toward the pursuit of a deeper personal walk with Christ, my new Lord. I was grateful for the confidence of God's people who urged me into wider and wider fields of service, and I recognized the need for it. Daily, I became more and more aware of how *much* Jesus needed disciples in whose very bodies He could walk the earth once more, ministering to His lost sheep. After having been one of those lost sheep for thirty-three years, my arms ached to take every troubled human being in the world to my heart, where I knew they would at least be close to Him who held my heart forever.

And yet, above the din of the world's need, above the definite call into a life of service, I heard the unmistakable high, clear notes of the call of His heart to mine: "Come unto *me* . . . Learn of *me* . . . Learn of *me!*"

I answered His call to my heart. In just three short years, I am learning to walk with Jesus, as the disciples walked with Him down the dusty roads two thousand years ago. This is no accomplishment of mine other than my willingness to seek *Him* before I sought greater fields of His service. It is a warm and wonderful feeling to share the fellowship of the blessed community as one after another of God's people clasp my hand in love and encouragement, but following Him into the deeper life means less of this and more hours of silence and weeping and crying out for mercy as one after another of my pet opinions and prejudices and abilities are cut into and changed and reshaped according to His intention. It is far easier to serve than to be changed. It is easier to speak from a platform than to be spoken to in the silence by the One who sees my heart laid bare. It is easier to write and direct an exciting dramatic radio program than it is to spend the cold morning hours on my knees being redirected by Him who alone knows His purpose for my life. But when I am altogether His, and walking minute by minute in His strength, He can automatically use me more because then and only then can He serve others through me. As long as I'm there, He can't get through, can He?

No, and if you have not discovered this in your own life, I beg of you to discover it now in the silence with Him, so that you too may say, "To me to live is not to *serve* Christ; to me to live *is* Christ!"

11.

To Me to Live
Is Not to
Be Christlike

In DIGGING into the depths of the meaning of Saint Paul's glowing testimony, "To me to live is Christ," we should seem to be able to come up with a conclusion right now and then move on to another thought. We should be able to tie it all up this way: if we say, "To me to live is *to be* or *to do* — *anything*," we are on the wrong track. The little infinitives should give us the key. And indeed in a general sense, they do. The very implication of the "to be" or "to do" shifts *us* into the place where, according to Paul, *Christ* must be.

And yet, there is one more "to be" which is so often used innocently when one is trying to let his or her life say, "To me to live is Christ," that I feel we must dig into this one before we move on. What is it? Just this: "To me to live is to be *Christlike!*"

Have you ever tripped over this one? I have many times. Those of you who, along with me, have been brought into a close, personal relationship with Christ out of another world, may have tripped over this rephrasing of Paul's famous line even more than those who have lived merely respectable Christian lives. Nevertheless, I feel quite sure that if we face facts honestly, we can all say that at one time or another in our Christian lives we have been absorbed with our own holiness. Or, we have become so preoccupied with checking up on our own spiritual growth that we have neglected or have completely forgotten that the Lord God said, "Feed my sheep" as well as "Be ye holy." We can become so taken up with wishful thinking concerning our own spiritual growth that without realizing it *we* are again in the center of our own lives and Christ and His purpose have been moved to the margins.

It is well to remember the familiar story about the little girl who kept digging up the seed she had planted to see whether or not it was growing. Disciples of Jesus Christ who become fascinated with their own potential resemblance to their Master slip dangerously near the brink of the so-called "new thought" cults. Absorption with our own holiness or our spiritual progress is *self*-development, isn't it? If Jesus did a finished work on the Cross, do we need to do more than stay in position to have His great redemption become a completed reality in our lives?

Please do not misunderstand me. I do not mean to imply that we must not "walk in the light as he is in the light," that we must not keep constant vigil over our relationship with Christ. I merely mean that those well-intentioned men and women who become impressed with their own growing resemblance to Christ *or* depressed by their growing lack of it are quite likely to put a sudden stop to the entire procedure. The living water will sink to a low level and stagnate. And we will wonder why when we have been giving such implicit attention to our own spiritual growth.

Did not our Master say we could not add one inch to our height by any effort of our own? Did He not say that He is the Vine and we are the branches? And did you ever hear of a branch clenching its leaves together in verdant agony as it pleaded with the vine to send down more sap? No.

The branch merely stays fastened on to the vine, and *expects* the supply of life-giving sap sufficient for its growth. The lilies and the tall green corn of the fields just stay in position to receive the sunlight and the rain and the nutriment from the soil.

Dr. Anna Mow (happily for me, my friend) gives this formula for one of those knotty, black days when we are inclined to put our spiritual conditions in the center of our attention. First of all, Anna checks whether or not she has had enough sleep the night before. If she has had, she checks the possibility that she has hurt someone inadvertently or intentionally. If this is not true, then she goes over the resentment and bitterness and self-pity departments. If all is well there and she can simply find no reason for her spiritual indigestion, she throws back her head and laughs her contagious, characteristic laugh and says: "All right, *you* stay here, Anna Mow, I'm going on with the Lord!" I've tried it too. It works.

God did say, "Be ye holy as I am holy"; but no amount of fascination with our holiness or lack of it will *increase* our holiness. He tells us to be holy, but then He sets about making us that way *when* we yield ourselves utterly into His lovely hands.

My dear friend and companion, Ellen Riley, twinkles with good-humored laughter at herself when she tells of her first years as a Christian. She was organist at the Methodist church back in our home town of Charleston, West Virginia. And so fascinated was she with the change in her personality after her conversion to Christ that she used to sneak long, admiring glances at herself in the mirror above the console of the big pipe organ on a Sunday morning as she sighed inwardly and thought: *Oh, isn't it wonderful? I'm growing more spiritual looking every day I live!*

This story always brings a relieved laugh from any group of Christians, because we are all guilty of becoming preoccupied in greater or lesser degrees with our own purity. And any movement of our *full* attention away from the face of Christ toward even our own Christlikeness is a dangerous and a confusing thing. It is risky for us and confusing for those who depend upon us. As glorious as holiness is when we see it actually happening in our own lives, we must not say, "To me to live is to be Christlike"; we must say and mean and then our very lives will proclaim "To me to live *is* Christ!"

12.

To Me
to Live
Is Christ

WE HAVE SEEN that it is an easy procedure for a well-meaning follower of Jesus Christ innocently to rephrase the singing words of Saint Paul: "To me to live is Christ." We have seen how easy it is to say, "To me to live is to be religious, to serve humanity, to serve Chirst, to be Christlike." We have also seen that any of these variations will result in sub-Christianity and an unvictorious life. Why? Because to a true disciple of Christ, his life is not a religion; it is the simple following of a living Person. And to him, this immortal testimony comes as naturally as breathing:

"To me to live is — Christ!"

So far as I know, I can claim this testimony as my own. *To me to live is the person of Jesus Christ.* And this is true for many reasons. Among them: I was not led into a *way of life* when I received Jesus Christ as my own personal Saviour and Lord and Master. I have dedicated this little book to the disciple of Christ who led me so carefully and so lovingly, *not* into a "better way of life," but into a close, intimate walk with the *person* of my new Lord.

I never think on the fact that I have found a better way

to live on this earth. But I think often and joyfully about the living Person who so recently drew me unto Himself — forever. I don't think, "Now, I can stay out of trouble"; but I live by the very fact of the Person who overcame my trouble on the Cross. I don't think, "Now, God will comfort me when tragedy strikes my life"; but I do rest in the tremendous knowledge that should tragedy strike, the person of the Holy Spirit will be right there to show me how to *use* that tragedy for His glory. I don't think, "Now that I'm a Christian, I won't drink anymore, or throw my money to the four winds and wind up deeper and deeper in debt." This is all true, but I don't dwell on that negative aspect of the whole thing. Instead, I just let the involuntary smile play away at the corners of my mouth because now that I belong to Jesus and He belongs to me, I don't *need* to drink. And I've *found* the fulfillment and excitement in Him, on which I used to have to spend my money. I don't think, "Now that I'm a Christian I must tithe and live conservatively"; I just return every dollar to Him at the outset and let Him spend it for me. "To me to live is Christ" because I was led, not into a better way of life, but into an intimate minute by minute walk with a living Person.

I have dedicated this book of discoveries to the one who convinced me *not* merely of a "plan of salvation" (I wouldn't have understood that phrase at all), but who *introduced* me *personally* to the Saviour, who did His own convincing in my heart and mind. As beautiful and as awe-inspiring as is the divine plan of God for the salvation of His lost sheep, it has little or no meaning for the pagan mind. Mine was a completely pagan mind, believing in nothing higher than my own wits. And so, the most careful intellectual or Scriptural explanation of the plan of salvation would have confused me; and since my pride would not allow me to admit confusion of any sort, any theological explanation of salvation would have only served to slam the door of the kingdom in my face.

But, thanks be to Christ, He had convinced my friend of His own *personal wonder.* He had drawn her to Himself out of a time of heartbreak and personal tragedy. She had found Him to be the living God with healing in His hands. She loved Him with all her heart when she met me, and she merely stood aside and let Him woo me unto Himself. "To me to live is Christ," because I was not merely intellectually convinced of a divine plan for the salvation of my eternal soul. I was permitted to fall in love with the Lover of my soul, Jesus Christ, the *living* Son of God.

This little book is dedicated to the disciple of Jesus Christ, who through her consecrated life allowed Him to confront me face to face with Himself. She did not attempt to frighten me into the kingdom by threatening me with an almost superstitious wielding of the written-down revelation of God, the Holy Bible. She knew I did not believe the Bible at all. And if she had had *only* Scripture texts (as dynamic as they are to me now) *then,* she would have been fighting a losing battle. She won me to Christ though, because she allowed the Holy Spirit full rein in *her* mind and imagination, and therefore guaranteed no blunders in timing. I was led gently and completely into a new life with Jesus Christ in a hotel room, and there was no one present with me but my friend, Ellen, and Jesus Christ.

After He had transformed me, then my desire for the wonder of the Holy Scriptures leaped into being; but if for some fantastic reason I should be told that the New Testament is all a mistake, I would still go right on following my living Lord. After all, the early Christians in the upper room had only the Holy Spirit Himself. If some reader decides from this paragraph that I do not believe with all my heart in the inspired Word of God as we have it in the Bible, I beg him to reread this meditation again more thoughtfully.

But to me to live is not the Bible, because the Word became flesh, not printer's ink; and as glorious as is that Spirit-inspired account of God's divine nature and plan, its light is to me the *person* of my Lord, Jesus Christ. Without reservation, "To me to *live is Christ*."

And this same Christ, available to me personally through His Holy Spirit, has proved Himself to me; so that I am not only a converted Christian, I am a totally *convinced* Christian, "strengthened with might by His Spirit in the inner man." Jesus Christ, the Holy Spirit and the Father have at last become One to me. And so, more than ever now, "To me to live is Christ," because all I need know of the Father is what He showed me in His Son.

Discoveries

Concerning a Number of
Wonder-filled Things

13.

Are
You
Free?

ARE YOU FREE? I know you live in a free country, but are you really *free?* I have lived in a free country since my first birth on June 22, 1916, but I have only been *free* since my second birth, October 2, 1949, when I was invaded from above and set free of my *self* by the transforming touch of the Holy Spirit.

This startling fact is almost humorous when I confess that most of those thirty-three years which passed between my first birth and my second birth were spent in loud protest against any kind of restraint and even louder declarations of personal freedom. I had to be free! I wanted everyone to leave me alone to live my own life as I wanted to live it — in freedom. I was a rebel from the word "go." I hated confinement and convention. I detested being disciplined. In fact to me "discipline" was the most unpleasant word outside of "obedience" in the entire English language, until I was thirty-three years old. Although my years numbered thirty-three, I had stopped growing emotionally at about a precocious sixteen. In my thirties, at the head of my own business, I was still asserting myself like an adolescent, kicking and yelling at life: "Leave me alone . . . I'm the type who just *has* to be free!" All this is too sadly true of some Christians who demand to remain the type that insists, "This is the way I am!" *Can't Jesus Christ change our natures?*

But back to freedom. In spite of the kicking and yelling for freedom all my thirty-three years, only *now* that I am at last free of my *self*, am I truly *free*. And, hold on to your hats, I found this freedom through *obedience* and *discipline!*

If we examine the inorganic matter in the bottom of a pool, we find it to be trapped there as dead matter. But, when that dead, inorganic matter is invaded from above by the root of a water lily, drawn up and *confined* within the disciplinary process of giving of itself to the lily, then and only then is that once-dead matter *free* to grow. Indeed, for the first time it is free to — live.

Not until I was invaded from above by the Holy Spirit was I free to live. "He that hath the Son hath life; and he that hath not the Son of God hath not life." Now, *drawn up* into the life of the Lily of the Valley, I am free to give of my once-dead self as nourishment to others. *Confined* in the glorious disciplinary process of giving of myself to Jesus Christ and His sheep, I am, for the very first time, free to grow.

Take the train off its track, and how far does it advance toward its destination? Suppose the engineer decides to indulge a sudden whim of his own and make the run between Chicago and Denver without a track to confine him. Will his passengers ever reach Denver?

Only in complete holy obedience to the merest whisper of Jesus Christ do we truly find the freedom for which we were created. And I firmly believe He created that desire for freedom within us all. The Father's heart grieves when His creatures are chained to earthly habits and beliefs. He created us to be free. And in Himself, through Christ, He provides that freedom.

A missionary friend of mine, a truly radiant Christian, once told me my life now reminded him of a flight he took over India some years ago. He smiled as he recalled the trip. It seems the pilot asked my friend if he would like to fly the plane, assuring him that if he did just as the pilot instructed, all would be well. The missionary agreed to try it. When the pilot said, "Pull this lever," he pulled that lever. When the pilot said, "Push this gear," he pushed that gear and so on.

"And sure enough," my friend beamed, "as long as I obeyed that pilot's every instruction, I was free to fly!"

My brother, the missionary, is right. My life is like that now. As long as I live every moment in obedience to the will of Christ — I am free to fly.

What are some of the things which rob Christians of their freedom? Surely, as we mention elsewhere in this book, *worry* is one of our most constant jailers. I believe that during the time we are worrying, we are actually atheistic. Either we believe Jesus Christ or we do not. He said, "I have overcome the world." Did He? Or is He playing a fiendish, cosmic prank upon us? I have, for a year or more, permitted myself the luxury of worry for five minutes at a time and no more. At the end of five minutes, if I am still worried, I go to the nearest mirror, look myself right in the eye and say, "This tremendous thing which worries you is beyond solution. Especially is it too hard for Jesus Christ to handle." Usually, I am restraining a laugh by that time, and when I let it go, the tears of gratitude come with the laugh, and I turn my eyes gladly back upon the face of Him who *gave* me a foolproof "worry-tree" in His Own Cross.

Worry, and fear and self-pity and bitterness and resentment and jealousy and temper and so forth and so forth and so forth can and *do* fence Christians in and prevent them from capering in the freedom Christ died to give us.

71

He died to set the alcoholic free from the bottle, and the dope addict free from the needle, but they are in the minority, and I wonder often at those of us who go about trying to save alcoholics when we are just as shackled to our sins of the spirit in the eyes of Him who *wants* us to be free.

I have discovered that God's spiritual laws are equally as reliable as His physical laws. If I jump out of a fourteen story window, I don't *break* the law of gravity. I just *illustrate* it. When we disobey God's laws, we don't break those laws. They're unbreakable. We simply illustrate them, as we break ourselves *over* those laws. A pilot who defies the laws of aviation crashes to the earth. He is no longer free to fly. Is the analogy so difficult to apply? Can we not see the freedom in obedience to Christ? Is Jesus Christ a God of His Word, or is He trying to confuse us?

I believe Him. And Jesus Himself said: "If the Son . . . shall make you free, ye shall be free indeed." The Son made me free; free to caper safely and unrestrainedly for the first time in my life, because I am *possessed* by the Holy Spirit of the One who created in me that longing for freedom. The Son of God has made me free, and I am free indeed.

14.

Are
You
in Love?

ARE YOU IN LOVE? Has your heart been touched by the hand of Him who alone knows the deeps of your heart? And has your heart responded? Has it responded to His voice? Has it been transformed by His touch? Has your heart been laid against His heart, there to stay forever?

Are you in love with the Creator of your heart? Are you in love with the Lover of your soul? Is He your Beloved and are you His? Now, this minute . . . tomorrow morning . . . tomorrow night and forever?

I am in love, and the plan of my love is very simple. To some it could be called my theology. To me it is simply the pattern of love. This is the pattern:

I belong to Christ and He belongs to me.

If you are not in love with Christ as you read these lines, surely you have been in love with someone in your life. And so you will know that when two are in love, the only true happiness for those two comes from being together. If we are separated from the one we love and know the time of reunion is near, don't we count the weeks, then the days, then the hours and then the minutes until we are together

73

again? Did not Jesus pray that we would be one with Him as He is one with the Father? That is the measure of His love for us. He wants not just to be near us, but to be *one* with us. And by His blessed Holy Spirit, He can literally indwell me. By His Holy Spirit, He can literally indwell *you*. He can be your Beloved and you can be His. He wants it that way. Do you?

Jesus of Nazareth, risen from the grave, went to sit at the right hand of the Father in heaven. But, oh, my soul trembles and my heart leaps at the wonder of knowing that although Jesus no longer walks the earth as the Man-God, He can still be present in an even more intimate and deeper sense through the person of His Holy Spirit within me. Out of the chaos of a hectic day, through the tense stillness of a sleepless night, the Voice within me whispers, "Peace, be still . . . I will never leave thee, nor forsake thee." In the midst of weeping, my broken heart is touched by the hand of Him who reminds me, "Lo, I am with you always . . . Let not your heart be troubled . . ."

How little we seem to know about love. How often we confuse love with lust or affection or self-love. Our divorce courts are crowded with men and women who want to be rid of each other because the other person didn't turn out to be the kind of ego-inflater he or she had promised to be. Men and women "fall in love" with their own ideas of what the other person should be. They "fall in love" with only the facets of the loved one's personality which happen to please them. I know this is true. In my B.C. days I was very "loving" to my friends who pleased me. So many tragic times we fall in love for what *we* can get from the relationship.

Close, constant contact with the One who *is* love shows us to our shame that love is giving and not receiving. I honestly believe I loved only one living creature unselfishly before Jesus Christ transformed me. I loved my English bulldog with as nearly an unselfish love as my unregenerate nature could muster. And her love for me? It charmed my life. It gave me, many times, a reason for waking up in the morning. I could desert her for hours, stay away from home until dawn, and instead of barking at me and taking me apart in fury when I finally came home, my doggy just about ate me up with joy because I had come back to her at last.

She taught me something about love. My mother's faith in me through the years taught me more about love. My father's loyalty to me no matter what he found out about me taught me still more about love. My brother's devotion to me in spite of the different worlds in which we lived taught me about love. But not until I met Jesus Christ face to face, did I meet Love as it was divinely created.

Divine love: There are no words to enlarge upon it. Nothing begins to describe it. It is complete in itself. It is — divine love. It has transformed my *self*-love into *other*-love. It has shown me the freedom of pouring myself out at the feet of Him who poured Himself out for me on the Cross. It has touched and transformed my possessiveness into a passion for being possessed by Christ. It has given me the freedom of not *needing* to love myself anymore. He loves me so much, I have no need for self-love, and this sets me free from self-pity, and self-defense, and self-assertion. If I am asked to go the second mile, I am free now to go gladly, knowing that en route, He will press even closer and bind me ever more securely to Himself in divine love.

I wonder at the men and women who follow the chilly reasoning of the cults which propagate the love *principle*. When a child wants its mother, it doesn't want the mother *principle*. It wants its mother's *arms*.

When my heart longs for the God for whom it was created, I do not want the God *principle*. I want the person of God. I want the divine Son of God, Jesus Christ.

DISCOVERIES

When I long for love, I could not be satisfied with the love *principle*. I want the everlasting arms of my Redeemer beneath me.

We must *surrender* ourselves utterly, we must *yield* ourselves completely. And yet, there is another word which I like even better than "yield" or "surrender." That word is "respond." It implies that He needs the response of *my* love to Him. It makes me feel needed. There is no sweeter emotion in all of life than to feel needed by one's beloved. My Beloved needs me and I need Him.

This same Beloved needs you, too. Does not your heart cry for Him? And will it not continue to cry out for Him until it comes to rest against His heart forever?

15.

Are
You
Satisfied?

ARE YOU SATISFIED and filled, or are you hungry and longing for more and still more of the wonder you have found
in Jesus Christ? At first thought, it would seem that the
Christian should answer, "Yes, I am completely satisfied."
And when the disciple is one with his Master, truly he *is*
satisfied. But still he longs for more.

We will return to this aspect of satisfaction in a moment,
after we have thought together about the restless kind of
dissatisfaction which seems to haunt the heart at night and
nip at the heels at noon. So many nervous, jittery Christians
dodge through life in much the same tense manner as the
non-believer, who must make a go of things by his own wits.

As we consider this tormenting dissatisfaction, we must
keep it separated from the healthy hunger about which we
will speak later on. If you are nervous, if your spiritual cup
is dry, if it has been a long, long time since you have had
anything to shout about where your Christian life is concerned, face yourself honestly under the searching eyes of
Him who promised to fill the hungry with good things. If
you are not filled, could it be that God has gone back on

His promise to you? Did He promise to fill you with good things and then did He get busy with some other celestial undertaking and forget all about you? Did He run out of living water before He reached your empty cup? If I am cross and restless and dissatisfied, does God have too many children to bless so that I can only reason that He must not be able to get around to blessing me today?

Does the Christ who said, "If any man thirst, let him come unto me, and drink," mean to go on depriving me of water for my spiritual life? Am I to go on worrying and fretting and stewing? Are you to go on being anxious and jealous and bitter? Are we to go on feeling sorry for ourselves because all around us others are bubbling over with living water and eating the bread of life?

Now, wait a minute . . . let's examine our side of the agreement. Assuming that we have made an eternal transaction with God on the basis of His redemption and have been reborn and given the power to become sons of God, are we keeping our side of the bargain? Are we spending enough time in the presence of God in silent adoration of Him? Are we feeding our minds and our hearts on the spiritual food in His Holy Scriptures? Are we working for God? Are we spending ourselves for Him? Are we "feeding His sheep"?

Are we?

Or, are we expecting a one hundred percent return from a twenty-five percent investment of ourselves? Of our time? Of our energy? Of our love? Frankly, I can't think of any person on earth who must be more miserable, more restless and more dissatisfied than a part-time, twenty-five percent Christian. If a man has just a little bit of religion, he can no longer enjoy the world's pleasures. He sits in abject misery in the midst of old worldly surroundings where once he reveled and where now he squirms. He sits in church or in a group with victorious, happy Christians and also — squirms. No matter where the poor fellow goes, he is a misfit. He is neither worldly nor Christian. He is divided. He lives in perpetual conflict. He is dissatisfied. And *only* a complete one hundred percent yielding of his life into the hands of the living Christ can calm his conflict, can unify him into one person again — a whole person, who can move toward a goal once more powered by the Dynamo of God, a man united within himself and with his Creator, a man at peace.

If you are restless and dissatisfied, no doubt you are two people trying to live one life. And it's a losing effort, until you unite *all* of you with *all* of Christ.

But what of those of us who are not *dis*satisfied, but who seem to be perpetually *un*satisfied? Is this good? Yes, this is healthy and a sign that we can be filled. We do not really enjoy a good dinner unless we are hungry, do we? So, if you are hungry for more and more of Jesus Christ, rejoice! The pains of hunger are His doing, I believe. He alone can make us want more of Him. He alone can create the hunger within us, just as He alone can satisfy that hunger.

It is very easy for the enemy to disturb us with anxiety over our spiritual condition when those healthy, normal hunger pains begin. He tells us that they are spiritual sickness, spiritual disease. We believe him and become discouraged, and he has the time of his evil life laughing at us as we writhe and agonize before God, begging to be filled when all we really need is to feast on Jesus Christ, the bread of life.

Are you unsatisfied? Are you still hungry? Good. Our Lord does not permit a single need in His children which He Himself cannot and will not fill. He longs to fill us with good things. The good things of the Lord stack up on the back stairs of our souls because we simply do not take them.

Let us rejoice in our hunger, all we who are children of

God, because He wants to feed His hungry children upon Himself, the eternal bread of life.

Isn't it wonderful to be hungry when we can feast on Jesus?

16.

Are
You
Worried?

ARE YOU WORRIED? How much time do you you spend each day worrying? How much time do you spend being afraid? Literally millions and millions of men and women are haunted night and day by fears, are nagged night and day by worry. For these millions life is one long desperate struggle; one long, futile search for some kind of peace of mind. Pitifully few ever find it.

What is worry? I have found two favorite definitions: "Worry is a cycle of inefficient thought whirling around a center of fear." Read and reread that definition, and its truth will make *you* stop short. First, because we all know of a certainty that worry does produce *inefficiency*. A worried mind is never an efficient mind. Then, the very use of the word "whirling" describes the usual behavior of one who worries. Move on in the definition now. "Whirling" around what? The wrong center. "Whirling around a center of *fear*."

"Fear thou not; for I am with thee . . . I will never leave thee, nor forsake thee."

Are we as Christians supposed to have Jesus Christ in the very *center* of our lives? Then, how is it that *we*, too, are guilty of "inefficient thought whirling around a center of *fear*"?

Another provocative definition of worry goes like this: "Worry is a chronic process of making mountains out of molehills." A Christian woman once looked a friend of mine right in the eye and said sincerely: "Well, if I don't worry, who'll hold things together?"

"Fear not; for, behold, I bring you good tidings of great joy . . . I will never leave thee, nor forsake thee."

With Jesus Christ in the center of our lives, how is it that we continue to worry?

Medical science has proved that literally thousands of illnesses are caused directly from worry and tension and anxiety. American Medical Association statistics tell us that well over *sixty percent* of *all* illness is caused by emotional, mental or spiritual disturbances. We know these things, and yet we continue to worry. Even Christians continue to worry. Our churches are pathetically populated with anxious Christians. *Nervous* Christians clutching doggedly and grimly at their doctrines and their problems instead of becoming "as little children" and resting in the Lord they profess to follow. Why do we do this? Isn't our faith big enough to hold us? Isn't our Lord strong enough to carry our burdens? Must we continue to worry them out ourselves?

"Come unto me, all ye that labour and are heavy laden [with fears and anxieties and worries], and I will give you rest."

We ask: *Is* there a *way out?* Is there a *way* out of fear and anxiety and worry for the tied-up human beings in this old world?

Coming home one night on a local train, I noticed a national magazine on the newsstand in the station. On its cover were splashed these words: NEW DRUGS TO EASE FEAR AND WORRY! I bought the magazine, and found that sure enough, science is gingerly offering a new drug called mephe-nesin which does, in many cases, offer blessed relaxation from nervous tension. The drug has aided in the improvement of patients with high blood pressure, heart trouble, alcoholism, asthma, etc. It has subdued that demon companion of the anxious — insomnia. A God-sent drug for a certainty. *But,* the article had a feeble pay-off. Science freely admits that this "anxiety fighter" (mephenesin) holds but one promise: It can show the victim what real relief from tension is. It said in effect that once having experienced the incomparable feeling of complete release and relaxation, many people will be able to go on from there to *achieve* true peace of mind and body.

This last statement made me want to sit right down and cry. One would think that people had to be talked into wanting relief from fear and worry and anxiety. That they only had to be convinced that they should try for it! Instead of sitting down to cry, however, I decided to write about this problem.

What have we said? "Worry is a cycle of inefficient thought whirling around a *center of fear.*" We have said that even Christians worry.

Now we ask some questions. Are not Christians supposed to have *Jesus Christ* in the center of their lives? And if so, how can *fear* be there too?

"Let not your heart be troubled . . . I am the good shepherd."

How can we as Christians worry about the fulfillment of our needs? How can we worry about financial matters? About clothes? About bank accounts? If our God is a God of His Word, how do we dare worry?

"Therefore I say unto you, Take no thought for your life, what ye shall eat, or what ye shall drink; nor yet for your body, what ye shall put on . . . Behold the fowls of the air; for they sow not, neither do they reap, nor gather into barns [bank accounts]; yet your heavenly Father feedeth them. Are ye not much better than they?"

Christians who worry must simply be Christians who have not yet gone the second half of the way with Jesus Christ. Christians are the only people on the face of this earth who can possibly escape worry; but only those Christians can escape who are willing to go the *second half* with Jesus, and say, "Yes, Lord, I have *You*, but more important *You* have me!" Those Christians have Jesus Christ straight and tall in the very *center* of their lives. Worry with them is an impossibility. A little boy doesn't worry if he's holding his father's hand, does he?

For our country and for us, the only *way out* of our inner turmoil of confusion and anxiety and worry and fear is the way of Jesus Christ who said: "Come unto me . . . and I will give you rest . . . Lo, I am with you alway . . . "

If we admit to spending even half an hour a day in worry, can't we promise our Lord we'll spend that half hour looking into His wonderful face, while standing steadfastly on His promise, "Seek ye first the kingdom of God, and his righteousness; and all these things [about which you worry] shall be added unto you"?

Jesus Christ is a God of His word. I know. I have tried Him and have found Him faithful. I have problems, yes. Some days they seem to come thicker than snowflakes in a Chicago blizzard. But thank God, I can honestly say these problems — large and small — *never* turn into *trouble*. I don't keep them long enough. I hand them right over to Jesus, who is always standing by waiting to take them. Standing by, keeping His promise:

"Lo, I am with you alway . . . "

17.

"Learn
of Me"

IF, FOR SOME FANTASTIC reason, I were to be suddenly forever deprived of every other passage in the Bible save one, I believe I would choose the last three verses of the eleventh chapter of the Gospel of Saint Matthew:

"Come unto me, all ye that labour and are heavy laden, and I will give you rest. Take my yoke upon you, and learn of me; for I am meek and lowly in heart: and ye shall find rest unto your souls. For my yoke is easy, and my burden is light."

In the Scofield Reference Bible, these three verses are called, "The new message of Jesus: personal discipleship." And since it is this all-compelling personal discipleship which must dominate our lives, if we are to be Christian in the true sense of the word, I feel a deep desire to share a few of my own somewhat recent discoveries concerning one particular line of this wonderful message of Jesus.

The everlasting invitation, "Come unto me, all ye that labour and are heavy laden, and I will give you rest," is a heart-call which no man or woman can resist, once his or her heart has truly been opened to it. But we would look now at the next line: "Take my yoke upon you, and *learn of me.*" A strong childhood memory of having heard that "take my yoke upon you" portion gave me the altogether backward, but unfortunately lasting, impression that the "yoke" of Jesus Christ was a burden in itself. A moment's thought will show how stupid an impression that was. Yokes are devices to lighten burdens. Jesus knew all about yokes, because He must have made them, many of them, with His own hands in the carpenter's shop. He knew they *helped* rather than hindered.

But leaving the "yoke," let's look squarely at the end of that sentence — "learn of me." A direct command of our Lord — "learn of me." As a new Christian, I am wide-eyed with wonder at the prospect of a lifetime . . . an eternity stretching ahead in which I will be able to learn of Him who so completely and wondrously transformed my life — top to bottom, inside and out. After thirty-three years of squeezing dry every situation and exhausting almost every person, I am overcome with adoration of a Lord whom I know I can never exhaust, and who not only says, "Learn of me," but helps me in the learning.

What is it to learn of Jesus Christ? In the beginning of my Christian experience I was convinced I knew all about Him. With a great sweeping gesture of abandon, I "sold all" and flung myself after Him, I thought! Now, I see that I didn't know Him at all. Quite suddenly He had invaded me, but I was still too blinded by my own "light" to see His face. Then, a little later on, when my own light began to die out, I was too dazzled by His light to see *His face* at all.

When we begin to be puzzled by Jesus Christ, I believe that is good. It is doubtful that He would ever turn out to be like our conception of Him. How could we conceive a Lord whose face is "set like a flint" and who stands like "an angel with tears in his eyes" at one and the same time? How could we conceive a Lord who "hath torn and [yet] will heal us? [Who] hath smitten, and [yet] will bind us up?" At these times of utter dismay about Jesus Christ, we feel we are being drowned in darkness. We begin to realize that there is a great distance between Jesus Christ and us. He is up ahead. We must run faster. We must pray more. We must spend more time with Him. Somehow, O God, somehow we must get closer to Jesus Christ! He is up ahead. He is up ahead. We cannot reach Him, and yet He said: "Learn of me!"

"How can I learn of you, Lord? Where will I begin?"

"If any man will come after me, let him deny himself, take up his cross daily, and follow me."

My Lord's answer: "Deny yourself, take up *your* cross daily, and follow me." Hard? Yes. Without His grace and His strength it is impossible. *With* Him "all things are possible." And delightful and greatly to be desired.

Even a cross? Yes. Because of His Cross our "cross" can be a joyful thing. Can there be joy in pain and suffering? For the true disciple of Jesus Christ, yes. But *only* for the Christian can this be so, because *only* the Gospel of Christ has a direct and effective way of dealing with suffering. By the grace and because of the suffering of Jesus Christ, the Christian is enabled not just to endure suffering; he can *use* it.

This is one of the recent things I have learned about Jesus Christ, in my somewhat stumbling efforts to obey Him when He says insistently: "Learn of me." On the next pages we will speak more of the way out of suffering. Not by escape, not by denial, but by redemptive *use* of whatever blows life deals us. A way out available *only* to those of us who follow the One who "took our sins into His heart and smothered them to death."

18.

What
About
Suffering?

THERE IS NOTHING so wonderful to the dedicated Christian as to think about Jesus Christ. I spend most of my available free time just *thinking* about Jesus. Nothing shortens a long train ride like thinking about Jesus Christ. Thinking about His gentleness, His almighty meekness, His tears, His deity . . . His lordship . . . His love . . . and all these things leave me sitting happily drowned in His grace. The never-ending, inexhaustible river of His grace. Never flowing away from me. Always flowing toward me. Always toward me . . . coming on, coming on, like a mighty river of love.

Thoughts like these set fire in the hearts of those of us who are His present-day disciples. But, even though Jesus Christ is first in many lives, and even though there are those who say gladly and joyfully, "Though he slay me, yet will I trust in him," still there are more who say, "What has He to offer me when *tragedy* strikes my life?" Or, "I know a wonderful Christian woman whose life has been cut into by tragedy at every turn! How is Christ the way out for her?"

What of all the horrible suffering in the world?

Where is Jesus Christ in all the suffering?

What does He offer as a way out of suffering?

What of the mental anguish inside the churches them-selves? What of the wars — mechanized, well-planned — and the bleeding and broken hearts they crush in their iron-hunger for spoils? What of the tragedy in the panic-wake of an earthquake or a volcanic eruption? Of tornadoes and hurricanes and floods? What of physical sicknesses, and the mental anguish that weeps along behind the thousands of funeral processions that move across our world each day? What of the suffering from poverty? From race prejudice? From jealousy? From possessiveness? From doubt? From fear?

What does Jesus Christ have to do with *all* heartbreak? If He is alive, if He really came out of that tomb, what part does He have in the *suffering* of His creatures? Does He simply sit at the right hand of the Father and look down with remote pity on us as we cry out, "Turn thee unto me, and have mercy upon me; for I am desolate and afflicted"? Is this the role of the Son of God in the suffering of His creations? What does Jesus really have to offer when we hear our own hearts break? When we listen to the breaking in the hearts of those we love?

If we worship ourselves as gods, in the time of suffering we turn to the most common form of dealing with it — self-pity. We derive pleasure from feeling sorry for ourselves. There is a touch of this in the fact that almost every man thinks his troubles and sorrows to be the greatest. Self-pity is one way to handle suffering.

Others among us turn to the ancient philosophy of Stoi-cism. This is the attitude of accepting suffering and inwardly steeling oneself to it. The old bloody-but-unbowed treat-ment. In a sense, this is admirable, but this very inward steeling turns invariably into hardness of heart. It is Stoic. Not Christian. In fact it is far, far from being Christian, and yet many Christians practice it. Many Christians smile through their tears and mutter between clenched teeth, "Well, I'll take it if it *kills* me! This thing won't get *me* down!" In such an attitude there is a touch of pathetic bravado, but not of genuine Christianity.

Buddha dealt with suffering and sin by declaring, "Existence and suffering are one. There can be no existence without suffering." And since *desire* causes the suffering and the sin, then the only sensible thing to do is to cut the root of desire completely. To lose one's identity in that passionless, actionless state called Nirvana is the Buddhist's way of handling suffering.

The Hindu *denies* the existence of all suffering and sin. He declares himself to be the divine and denies that anything whatever is wrong.

The Moslem lies submissively under the whip hand of sin and suffering and declares all of it to be God's will. This attitude is also shared by many who think themselves completely Christian. How often have you heard someone say in the face of some tragedy: "Well, we'll just have to accept this as God's will"? Christians say this firmly believing that they *know* the nature of Jesus Christ who said: "I am the good shepherd: the good shepherd giveth his life for the sheep." Would a God who said this Himself actively *will* for a baby to be burned to death? No. Suffering is in the world because of sin and evil. Not because it is God's will. And we as Christians must realize and proclaim loudly in our actions that Jesus Christ, our Lord, and *only* Jesus Christ offers a *way out* of suffering. It is a sure *way out* because He and He alone showed us by example how to *use* suffering. Can anything that happens to us be worse than what happened to *Jesus?* And didn't He *use* the Cross to save us?

All other religions deny suffering or dodge it in some manner. The religion of Jesus Christ uses it. The Holy Spirit can and will take your suffering and transform it into good.

This is not idle philosophy. This is fact. Radiant Christians' step from prison camps where they have seen their own families murdered before their eyes. How is this possible? Because our Lord accepted the fact of human suffering instead of dodging it. He accepted it and made ready the one and only way of using it redemptively. He did not bring a philosophy. He brought a fact. The fact of Himself. By the very act of allowing His own dear body to be broken on the cross, He took the world's greatest tragedy and turned it triumphantly into the world's greatest testimony! He did not just bear things; He *used* them.

This same Jesus Christ is alive today in all His resurrection power with this practical *way out* of all our human suffering. And He does not expect us to do it alone. He explains little; but if we are willing, He will change anything.

He will take your suffering and your sin into His own heart again right now, and there He will transform it into goodness and joy for you. And best of all, out of your suffering will come a new awareness and new nearness to Jesus, the Christ of God.

I know this to be true. I have discovered it for myself as He showed me how to use a personal tragedy about which I could not even speak. I am grateful that I was not permitted the luxury of sympathy. I *had* to turn to Him alone. Now He has turned my suffering into joy. And scarcely a day goes by that He does not use it at least in some small way.

19.

Listen to
What He
Has to Say

IF A NEW ACQUAINTANCE asked you the question, "With whom do you live"? what would you reply? Would you say "Oh, I live with my mother, my father and my brother"? Would you say "I live with my husband and my three children?" Or "I live with my wife and four kids, one dog and two canaries"?

No one else? No other Person in your home? Or is He there, but shut away in a dark closet, unable to be a part of the fun in the family, unable to share the warmth around the fireplace in winter, or the cool expectancy of a spring evening daringly spent on the front porch ahead of all the neighbors? Is Jesus Christ shut away in a closet of your home? Can't He come to dinner with you? Can't He converse with you? Is He being deprived of all the *joy* in your *home?* If this is true, then how can we expect to be able to remember where we've hidden Him when *tragedy* strikes our home?

Jesus Himself said: "Learn of me." How can we learn of someone whom we never see? With whom we never have intimate conversation? With whom we never laugh? *To whom we never listen?*

Who is this Jesus Christ who dared to say: "I am the way, the truth, and the life"? Who is this Jesus Christ whom we declare to be the only way out?

"I am the Lord . . . Look unto me, and be ye saved, all the ends of the earth: for I am God, and there is none else." A few short years ago, before my conversion to Jesus Christ, I would have argued: "But how do I know He is God? How do I know?"

"Be still, and know that I am God."

"Be *still*, and know that I am God . . . Learn of me." It is my observation that few Christians take time to be silent and listen to God. How can we obey Him if we do not hear His voice? The Scriptures give us a general plan for guidance, and surely we should take no step which in any way contradicts God's inspired written Word. But, what of the particular times of confusion and indecision which spring from particular circumstances in our own individual lives? The only possible way we can be sure that we are obeying God in these instances is to know Him. To know His character. To know God Himself, as He has revealed Himself through the person of our Saviour and our Lord, Jesus Christ. We can learn much about Jesus Christ personally from learning what He has done in other lives. And yet, this gives us only what the study of theology gives us — knowledge of things *about* Jesus. I would know Him personally. I *must* know Him personally. And so I obey Him when He says: "Be still, and know that I am God."

From the very first morning following my conversion to Jesus Christ, October 2, 1949, I have faithfully kept a "quiet time." I read the Bible, perhaps some devotional book other than the Bible, and then sit for at least half an hour in silence before God. I have been in the homes of ministers during the past two years where I was privileged to share the morning devotions before catching a train. The procedure went something like this: The minister or his wife read from the Scriptures, perhaps one of the children sang, perhaps we all sang (there can never be too much singing!), then usually the minister prayed. And then? Well, then he got briskly to his feet and said, "Now let's be about the business of the day!" I do not mean this in a critical spirit. I am simply puzzled. Because I could not . . . would not *dare* face a day without the fresh infilling of the Holy Spirit during that time of being *quiet* before God when it is morning.

When we go to a doctor we sit down before him and tell him what hurts us. We tell him the symptoms. We ask his advice. *Then* what do we do? Do we dash out the door already intent upon our next bit of business, pleading with the doctor to help us after we are well out of his sight, perhaps down on the street hailing a taxi or waiting for a bus? No, we wait quietly for the doctor's advice. We not only wait for it, we *expect* it. Can he cure our ailment if we don't hear his diagnosis and his remedy?

I think the analogy is apparent. I prayed earnestly for a year for the salvation of one very dear friend, and then one day God managed to get through my much talking with a divine nudge to "Be still, and know that I am God." I fell silent finally. I waited. And in a day or so I realized full well that I had many restitutions to make before that friend could possibly see Jesus Christ through me. Since I was the only plausible link between her and God, I had to set about making those painful restitutions at once.

Surely we can come to know Jesus Christ personally in no better way than being quiet before Him. Time spent in feeding our inward lives with His lovely presence will ultimately make it possible for us to carry this inner life out into the market place. Time spent in silence before God teaches us what it really means to "pray without ceasing." We come to live on two levels at once. The calm of the deep, quiet, unchanging inner level where we are Christ's and Christ is God's, where the pool of His peace is never disturbed by any tornadoes blowing from without, will begin to be felt in the bustle and turmoil of our exterior lives. Those who spend time with us will not only know that we "have been with Jesus," but that we *are* with Jesus. Our very lives will speak for Him, because the living God will speak through our lives to an anguished, frightened world: "Come unto me . . . Look unto me, and be ye saved . . . I and my Father are one . . . be still, and know that I am God."

20.

"I Am
the Door" (I)

I FIND ONE FRAGMENT of Scripture coming again and again, and so I will set down this fragment, and allow it to lead us down still another path of discoveries about Jesus.

"I am the door: by me if any man enter in, he shall be saved, and shall go in and out, and find pasture . . . Verily, verily, I say unto you, He that entereth not by the door into the sheepfold, but climbeth up some other way . . ."

What other *ways* are there? How do we dare choose another way beside the way of the One who declared and got a world to believe that "I am the way, the truth, and the life"? How do we dare go against the One who also declared: "I am the door"?

What other ways of facing life are there? Too many to list. But commonly, there is the way of *resentment*. There is the way of *escape mechanisms*. There is the way of *self-defense*. There is the way of *materialism*. There is the way of *fear*. There is the way of *pleasure*. But do these ways lead to a victorious life? No, they lead to — nothing. They are dead-end ways. They are blind alleys. And yet we, the blind, lead the blind up and down these alleys daily, refusing the *one* way out. Refusing even to try the door.

The famous nerve specialist, Dr. Walter Alvarez, says: "I often tell patients that they cannot afford to carry grudges or maintain hates or resentments. Such things can make them ill and can certainly tire them out. I once saw a man kill himself, inch by inch, simply by thinking of nothing but hatred of a relative who had sued him. Within a year or two he was dead." God has fashioned us for love. Not hate. For love. Not resentment. "Love is our native air." Anything else is poison. Surely the way of resentment is a rough road with a dead-end. The only *way out* of resentment permanently is by the cleansing and redemption of the One who offers Himself as the door.

Then there are the ways of *escape mechanisms*. Among those ways most struggled along are the winding, endless catacombs of *alcoholism* and *sensationalism*. Just as one drink for the alcoholic usually leads to two, so one sensation tried leads to boredom and the pursuit of still another sensation. The door out of those twisting tunnels of darkness? There is only one way . . . one door of release. Jesus tells us: "I am the way . . . I am the door."

There is another well-traveled way with a dead-end: the way of *self-defense*. "I've got a right to stick up for my rights!" But Jesus said: "He that findeth his life shall lose it: and he that loseth his life for my sake shall find it." We stand our ground and scream: "I'll fight for my rights!" Christ says: "If any man will sue thee at the law, and take away thy coat, let him have thy cloak also."

Another popular way of life is the way of *materialism*. We are a material-mad race of people. Build, increase, expand, pile up, hoard. More and more and more. "If we can just make enough money to — to — !" Jesus said: "Sell that ye have, and give alms; provide yourselves bags which wax not old, a treasure in the heavens that faileth not, where no thief approacheth, neither moth corrupteth."

Still another way is the shadowy way of *fear*. No one consciously chooses this way. But anyone can leave it behind forever. An ancient Persian saying contends: "Worry eats up the human flesh." Medical science says, "So does fear." In Mark 4:19 we see that: "The cares of this world . . . choke the word, and it becometh unfruitful." One writer declares, "Not only do care and fear and worry 'choke the word,' they choke the person too!" It is a well-known medical fact that fear-ridden patients are easily choked. They are shallow breathers. What is the way out of the way of fear? There is only one. The One who declared: "*Fear* not, little flock; for it is your Father's good pleasure to give you the kingdom."

There is also the *way of pleasure*. This so-called way leads perhaps more quickly and more heartbreakingly to a dead-end than any other. I know. I tried it for some fifteen years. Tried it skillfully. Carefully. Expensively. Imaginatively. Diligently. And ultimately — despairingly. The *pursuit of pleasure* occupies the minds and spare hours and energies of nine out of ten men, women and children in this vast land of ours. No one loves a good time more than I do. And I thank God that at last . . . at long last, I have learned the art of having a good time "in the midst of." A trip to a particular place no longer guarantees a happy vacation for me. I will have joy and the "peace that passes all understanding" if my vacation doesn't pan out as I have planned it in any detail. Why? Because Jesus will be wherever I am . . . giving His joy minute by minute by minute . . . "in the midst of."

People shout: "We wanta' have fun our way!" Jesus says: "These things have I spoken unto you, that *my* joy might remain in you, and that your joy might be full."

"These things have I spoken unto you . . . I am the door

. . . no man cometh to the Father but by me . . . I am the door . . . I am the way, the truth, and the life."

We who have tried to climb up some other way have found unmistakably and forever . . . that Jesus Christ *meant* every word He said.

21.

"I Am
the Door" (II)

JESUS SAID: "I am the door." What did He mean? Obviously He meant much more than we know about. But think for a moment about doors themselves. We think of a door as an article which opens *into* or out of something. A door leads from something to something. A doorway leads from one room to another. Jesus said: "I am the door." He also said: "I am the way." Jesus Christ, then, unless He lied, actually leads from one state to another. We can agree on this.

What, according to psychologists (*and* according to what we know of ourselves) do we, as human beings, fear or dread above all other phenomena? What would we avoid if we could? Here are four major "dreads" which, if man could pass through, or avoid, he would, I believe, be free from most of his fear:

First, *death*. We fear death for many reasons. God has planted in every living thing the desire to live. Even the tiniest bug will struggle for life when faced with death. Injured men will crawl for miles for life-saving aid, fearing, dreading death. Psychologists say, "Every man in his right mind wants life." And yet, there is nothing . . . nothing so certain, so absolutely inevitable as *death*. Birth may fail. Never death. *But wait* . . .

". . . whosoever believeth in *him* should not perish, but have *everlasting* life."

If we are to believe Jesus Christ, if we are to believe the inspired word of God as we read it in His Word, the Holy Bible, we are faced with a startling statement: "I am the door . . . I am the way . . . [to] everlasting life"!

Did Jesus Christ mean what He said? Was it all true? *Is* it still true? If it is not, He was the most shocking deceiver who ever walked this earth. But He was not. It is true.

From my own experience, I know I have found the door which leads from *death* into *eternal life*. I have been found by the One who said: "I am the resurrection and the life." Jesus cancels the fear of *death* by His *life*.

We look now at dread number two, *failure, defeat*. No one wants to be a failure. There is nothing to celebrate in failure. Celebrations go with victories. No one wants or seeks failure . . . and society as a whole does not love a man who is a failure. We fear *failure*. We dread *defeat*. The alcoholic who sits dejectedly before his half empty bottle, after having sworn off forever, knows the abject humility and pain of *defeat*. The mother who watches her son being led away to prison knows the heartbreak of personal failure. The schoolboy lags behind his classmates as they leave for home the last day of school; the blood is pounding in his head from the humiliation he feels because *his* report card reads: Failure. No one walks through life without major *and* minor defeats and failures. But wait . . .

Jesus said: "I have overcome the world." And dear aging John, the disciple Jesus loved, drew on the strength of His Lord to declare: "Whosoever believeth that Jesus is the Christ is born of God . . . [and] whatsoever is born of God

overcometh the world: and this is the victory that overcometh the world, even our faith." Surely, Jesus Christ *is*
the door from *defeat* to victory.

Dread number three is the dread of *bondage*. Of not
being *free*. America is built upon the belief in freedom.
And yet, no nation can guarantee personal freedom to its
people. Personal freedom from the bondage of self and
sin and the inevitable circumstances of life *must* come from
above and be worked out *within* each individual life. We
have seen radiant Christians chained to their wheel chairs.
We have been guided by radiant Christians with sightless eyes. We have watched bed-ridden Christians "mount
up with wings as eagles." Why? How? Because they
have walked by faith through the door to — freedom.

Jesus said: "If the Son . . . shall make you free, ye shall
be free indeed."

Lastly, man's fear and dread of *insecurity* can rule and
ruin his entire life. There are two ways of meeting this fear
on the human level. We can lay up material security, or
we can deny the need for it. Both ways are false. But the
man or woman who, like Paul, has "learned both to abound
and to be in want" is truly free of this black dread of insecurity forever.

. . . When you have stopped reading, I beg you to spend
several minutes in quiet contemplation before this One who
dares to say: "I am the door" which leads *away* from *defeat,
bondage, insecurity* and *death,* and "I am the way" which
leads *to* victory, freedom, security and eternal life.

22.

Where Is
Jesus Christ?

WHERE IS JESUS CHRIST?
Where would one find Him in your life? Where do *you* find Him? Do you have to travel to some particular place? Do you have to do some particular thing?

Where do you go to find Jesus? Where do you go to be sure of the presence of God? In all ages, religion has been associated with sacred places. Thousands drag their sick and weary bodies to the banks of the Ganges river, so they may die in sight of this sacred stream. A friend of mine, a missionary, once saw a Mohammedan saying his prayers on a train. The Mohammedan knelt upon his prayer mat on the floor of the train and tried to face toward Mecca. I say he *tried* because the train happened to be spiralling up a twisting mountain track, and the poor Mohammedan had to resort to a compass placed on the floor in front of him so that he could keep turning his body in a rather frantic effort to keep facing the holy place.

Does this make you smile? Well, where do *you* find Jesus? How do *you* contact God?

You may have read, as I have, of the Indians of Latin

America who take long pilgrimages to a sacred shrine made in the image of Christ. But as they leave, they are heard to cry: "Adios, Christos! Adios, Christos!" — "Good-bye, Christ! Good-bye, Christ!"

They leave Christ standing there trapped in that sacred shrine, as they walk away tearfully waving good-bye to the One who died that they might *be one* with Him forever.

Where do you find Jesus Christ? In church you say? Yes, so do I. But what about the moment when you walk out the front door of your church and down the steps toward home? Does Jesus go along with you, or do you leave Him behind — trapped in the stained glass window or shut until next week between the airless pages of the Psalter resting in the church pew where you sat?

Before I received Jesus Christ as my Saviour and Lord I thought of these two words, "sacred" and "secular," as being poles apart. And now, when I look about at God's children from within the warm, safe encirclement of His everlasting arms, I am hurt and many times bewildered that so many of His followers only follow Him part of the way. The dividing line between their *sacred* and their *secular* is wide and sometimes uncrossable.

I knew the utter darkness of a life of atheism. I am Christ's now. I am spared the struggle of indecision, the agony of choosing and the throes of the double-walk. I simply follow Jesus and take my strength from His Holy Spirit which dwells within me. I tremble at the turmoil which rushes toward me like a black and angry monster when I step off the "holy highway" of obedience to Christ.

I wonder and sometimes marvel at the human fortitude of Christian believers who manage to live both a secular and a sacred life. I marvel at those who can leap back and forth across that darksome gap between trips to church from week to week. I do not speak of worldly indulgences now;

I merely speak of those who leave Jesus Christ in the pews when they leave their churches.

I have found Jesus Christ to be directly interested and quite personally involved with me in every line I write. I am firmly convinced that Jesus Christ is interested in our vacation plans, our recreation time, our fun. I have a devout friend who lives in His presence from minute to minute, who once had his early morning devotions broken while on a fishing trip. A large fish nearly jerked the pole out of his hand. He landed the fish, and went on with his prayer. "There didn't seem to be a real interruption," he said later. "The Lord was interested in my fishing trip." I believe this. This man belongs to Christ completely. Why wouldn't Christ be interested in his fishing trip? Can't we take God into everything? To take Him into everything does not mean that we lower *Him;* it merely means that we *lift our lives!* To take God into our pleasures does not mean that we make Him commonplace. I believe it means that we allow Him to make our pleasure *un*common.

As I write these words I am beginning the fourth year of my walk with Jesus Christ. I have discovered many things. I have been given a completely new life. Not one of the least exciting discoveries I have made, however, is this: When I determined to take Christ into my every pleasure, I found the *one sure way of finding out* just what a Christian can and cannot do and still remain true to the Person whom he follows!

And so, as an extremely happy and joy-filled and delighted Christian of three years (at this writing), I want to go on record as saying that I believe no Christian has a right to take part in *anything* into which he or she cannot walk wholeheartedly with Jesus Christ. We can just toss out the two words "secular" and "sacred" from our vocabulary from now on, and rejoice as we gladly call it *all* — His.

23.

Your Talent,
Yes, But
You Too

"Jesus Christ does not want your talent. He wants *you!*"
I have dashed several young (and not so young) hopefuls full in the face with this seemingly blunt and discouraging statement. I don't enjoy seeing my words wipe smiles away and furrow brows of these would-be Christian writers, actors, musicians, singers, producers, directors, et cetera, ad infinitum. It is embarrassing, in fact, since at the moment I am earning my living as a Christian writer, director and producer.

I cannot, however, but believe this is the truth concerning the question of service: "Jesus Christ does not want your talent. He wants you!" After all, upon facing the matter squarely, doesn't giving yourself entirely to Him *include* your talents too? Now, perhaps you are saying: "Well, what's all the fuss about then? Isn't it all the same in the final analysis?"

No, it is not the same. It is a fearful and dangerous thing, I believe, for a disciple of Christ to decide *how* Christ is to use his or her talents. It would seem that if one is blessed with a lovely voice that he or she should serve God as a singer. Or a writer, if he or she can write. Or as an artist, if he or she can paint. But I am forced, by my own firm conviction and by the results of my own experience, to insist that Jesus meant what He said when He said: "Come unto *me!*"

He didn't say, "Bring your talent unto me." He said, "*You* come yourself!" To me it makes all the difference in the world which comes first. If we bring the talent first — even if we offer it completely — we are holding onto the right to ourselves. If we say, "Lord, here is my lovely singing voice, I would use it for Thee," we are, as a friend of mine says, "making a cosmic errand boy of God." We are directing Him.

But, if we come to Him first, holding out empty hands, offering ourselves *and* the right to ourselves, then and only then can Jesus Christ make *full* use of our talents to the *glory of Himself.*

I know this to be true. I tried it.

Some three years ago, when I surrendered my life into the hands of the living God, I said to myself dramatically (and quite naturally): "You have been a successful writer for ten years in the service of the enemy of God. Now you must give your years of experience and your talent to Christ, perhaps to write *the great* Christian novel!"

I have to smile now, remembering my spiritual blindness in those first, eager days in the kingdom. Jesus Christ knew about the talent. And He knew what use He might have for it — *in the future.* But He also knew that He had a still stubborn, still carnal, still unbroken newborn creature on His hands. She was waving her arms and saying: "I will serve Him with *my* talent," and He was holding her in His hand patiently awaiting the moment when she quieted down enough for Him to get a word in too.

He could not use her talent until He had her completely.
Gradually, over the strange new months of that first year,

as I began to get closer and closer to the person of Jesus, I said less and less about "the great novel." I thought less and less about "writing for God" and more and more about *knowing* Him personally. Slowly this began to dawn on my newly awakened consciousness concerning things as they *are* in the kingdom of God: My business was *not* to serve Jesus Christ. My business was to *belong* to Him utterly and completely and without one single reservation. Then, and only then, could He trust me with His service.

Isn't it easy for us to decide *for* God about how we are to serve Him? Isn't it easy for us to satisfy our own egos by cloaking our personal ambitions in the language of God, and arranging the spectators and the setting to suit our own ideas of our own merits and capabilities?

Yes, it's more than easy. It's *natural.* But the power with which we reckon as Christians is *supernatural,* and so it is not for us to consecrate our gifts to God. They are not ours to give.

Ours is not to decide; ours is to belong. Ours is to do the will of Him we adore. And He said: "If any man will come after me, let him deny himself, take up his cross daily, and follow me."

"Follow *me*," not a particular form of service for which we seem fitted. "Follow *me!*" And we can only follow Him according to His will by drawing ever closer to Him in our daily lives. Not closer to a religion, but closer to the altogether lovely person of Jesus Christ. We cannot please a friend completely unless we know that friend's every wish. And so, let us open our minds and wills and hearts to Him, asking Him, by the Spirit of truth, to teach us more and still more about Him*self.* Because the more we know of Jesus as He is, the less we are concerned with our own personalities except that they be caught up in the light of the personality of the One whom we serve — not for the sake of serving, but because we belong.

You say: "But if I am born with a talent, isn't it just common sense that I use it for God?" No, not necessarily. If common sense had been enough, Jesus would not have had to die.

Is that true? Yes.

If common sense had been enough, Jesus Christ would not have had to die.

24.

The Difference Between "Life" and Life

WE'VE ALL HEARD the expressions, "I want to *live!*" or "A man only *lives* once, so I'm going to make the most of every minute!" I have not only heard both expressions; I have used them time and time again . . . *before* I found out what *life* really means. What *living* really means.

"I am the way, the truth, and the *life*. No man cometh unto the Father but by me . . . whosoever believeth on me, shall have everlasting *life* . . . he who hath the Son hath *life*."

Before grasping the eternity of difference between "life" and *life*, we have a tendency to squeeze the last drop from every experience. A good interlude, such as an absorbing book or an enjoyable concert, or a happy vacation time can make us feel that "life" is good. We hang onto each ephemeral moment of these happy times and say, "If only this could go on — this is really living!"

Well, that *is* living a "life." But we must find *the life*, and "this is life eternal, that they might know thee the only true God, and Jesus Christ whom thou hast sent." And, to *know* God as revealed to us in His Son, Jesus, is to *have* eternal life. A *life*, which is not only for some future time, but a *life* which begins the very instant a man or woman turns the reins of his or her existence over to the Son of God.

At thirty-six years of age, I have finally found that under our own steam — searching about wildly as we may — we cannot *live* through earthly power. Nor through chemical power (including all the artificial stimuli known to mankind). Nor can we *live* through human power: physical, intellectual, emotional or will power. The only power by which we can find life is the power promised by Jesus to all believers . . . that inexhaustible, dynamic enduement of power that comes to us the moment the Holy Spirit comes in to take over in our stead.

Only one or two Christians (including the clergy) have been able to give the writer (a new Christian) a realistic definition of the Holy Spirit. Some theological explanations have stimulated the mind, but I am overjoyed to report that the Holy Spirit Himself has revealed *Himself* to me in a new and vital way. The Holy Spirit has ceased being "It" and has become *He!* The Spirit of truth is come . . . he will guide . . . into all truth.

The Holy Spirit is not a freak of God nor a spasm of the divine nature, nor a pocket edition of Jesus Christ. He is not a mere influence nor the inspiration of a poet or teacher. He is a divine Personality, an almighty Being who has a will, an intellect and a heart. He Himself must live in us or there is no more divine power in us than in others. He Himself must move in us or we are helpless. He Himself must speak through us or else our words will be "as the babbling of fools or the crackling of thorns under a pot."

When Pilgrim started his progress away from the City of Destruction he cried, "Life, Life, more Life!" Too much of our cry today is, "Work, work and more work." Or, "Service, service and more service." Or, "Funds, funds and more funds." Or, "Crowds, crowds and more crowds."

In my own personal life I have discovered as an irrefutable

truth that unless the presence of the Holy Spirit of God goes along with my progress away from my "city of destruction," I will cry helplessly against a canvas sky . . . and hang my highest hopes on no loftier summit than the point of a cardboard moon.

The Holy Spirit manifests Himself in us in the "more abundant life." And life can only be defined as — life. We cannot analyze it, imitate it or create it. A professor at a large western university once took a common squash and put it in a steel case. On the lid of this steel case, he placed a one hundred pound weight. The squash grew and its *life* lifted the hundred pounds. He then put on a two hundred pound weight. The squash lifted the added weight. The professor then put on five hundred pounds of weight. The squash grew and up went the five hundred pounds. Then on went an anvil and a piece of railroad iron. And the life-filled squash plant broke the steel case to pieces!

If God can put that much power in a squash, what amount of power can He put into a disciple of His Son, Jesus Christ? And what potent kind of *life* can we as disciples send out into all the darkened world, if we but turn completely to the *life* for which we were created?

Why *waddle* along through "life" when we can *soar* through *life?*

25.

What Is
in the Center
of Your Life?

WHAT IS IN THE VERY CENTER of your life? If we follow
Jesus Christ, it would seem the answer would be obvious.
We should be able to say without hesitation: "Why, Jesus
Christ is in the center of my life."

But can we say this and feel certain our statement will
stand up under close investigation? As one so lately a
member of the pagan world, and as one so deeply concerned
that other pagans are allowed to see Christ as He really *is*,
and so come into His kingdom joyfully, as I came, I beg of
you to look closely at your life as we come to the closing
pages of this book of discoveries about the person of Jesus
Christ.

On the absolute childlike belief that He meant every
word He said, I stake my eternal life on the fact that if
Jesus Christ is lifted up — *as He* really *is* — He will draw
all men unto Himself! He said He would, and I believe
Him. And with this promise of His in our hearts, let us face
clearly some of the innocent, unconscious habits of thinking
into which Christians fall; habits which turn *away* non-

believers when the sincere desire of the Christian's heart is to bring them *into* the wonderful light.

I believe these habits can all be summed up under the heading of "too much self-effort." And this is why I say that we get so carried away with wanting to serve Christ that we leap in and try to do His work for Him. I have spoken at some length earlier about the gentle, simple way in which I was brought into the glorious personal walk with Jesus Christ. And I want to emphasize for the sake of clarity, and for Jesus' sake, that there is *no one set way* of leading a man, woman or child to Christ. Our part is merely to "lift Him up" and let Him do His own work.

In the portion on the viewpoint of Christ, we discussed this in detail. But now, we should look at just a few of the *right* endeavors which we put in the *wrong* places in our Christian lives.

First of all, Jesus did say, "Go ye into all the world and make disciples." And any effort on our behalf to lead another human being into a saving knowledge of Jesus Christ is one of the vital roots of a Christian life. *But,* how many of us put "soul-winning" in the very center of our lives and thus go about tight-lipped and tense, *hiding* Jesus Christ behind our own anxious natures, instead of "lifting Him up"? Again, I ask you to *think* as you read these lines. They can be so easily misread. No one among you thrills more to the pure joy of bringing a stray sheep home to the Shepherd than I do. I know how lonely and lost it feels to be out there in the world without Him. I know what a desperate feeling it is to have the universe end with the top of one's own head. But, if I allow my desire to "win others" to settle in the center of my life, Jesus Christ has to move to the margins. I become tense and nervous when the days go by without my having brought anyone to Christ, and before I know it, I am hiding Him from the world behind my own anxiety.

We must keep Christ Himself in the center.

We need only stay in position to be used. We need only to do as the lilies do. Wouldn't we pity the poor apple blossom that cried to bear an apple of its own effort? But we needn't pity the poor apple blossom, because it is wise enough to stay in position on the branch until the apple is born *through* it.

It is easy for well-meaning, sincere Christians to put soul-winning in the center of their lives, so that Jesus Christ is moved to the margins. But if He is in the center, dominating our thoughts, calming our fears, erasing our anxiety, *balancing* our lives, He will keep His word and draw others unto Himself — *because* of Himself.

It is also easy for well-meaning, sincere Christians to put "witnessing" in the center of their lives. We hear well-intentioned admonitions to witness daily for our Lord. But if I talked about Jesus Christ simply because I thought it was my duty to talk about Him, secretly I'd begin to resent the whole thing in no time. I am not ashamed to admit this. It is a simple fact. On the other hand, when we are so in love with Christ, so completely convinced that even if there were no eternal reward when we leave this earth, *His* is still the most fulfilling, the most exciting, the most joyful way of life, *then* we talk about Him because we just can't help it. I have asked myself this question for many months and at last I can answer it in the *affirmative* with no hesitation:

> *If* for some reason Jesus Christ came to me and said that He had made a big mistake, that there was no eternal reward, and no heaven and no hell — would I still follow Him?

Would you? Can you answer that right now with a quick, uncompromising "Yes"? If you can, then you do not worry about when and where you will be called upon or permitted the chance to witness. You will just talk about Him be-

115

cause you are so full of Him you can't help doing it. I have heard sincere Christians pray for the "opportunity" to witness. Every breath we take is that opportunity. Every cab ride, every dinner out, every bus ride, every guest who drops in, every time the front door bell or the telephone rings — we are swamped with chances to talk about Jesus. Now, I do not mean to imply that we must clench our fists and set our jaws and force a word about Him *every* time we brush another human being. That, in fact, is my point. If we force ourselves to witness, then we are putting our *duty to witness* in the center, and over into the margin of our lives must go our Lord.

Just as we can put service to Christ, to humanity, to our churches in the center, so we can put winning others and witnessing in the center. I believe *all* these are the fruits of *belonging* entirely to the *only* One who has the right to stand forever in the very center of our lives — Jesus Christ.

26.

Easter

WHEN I WAS A CHILD of about seven or eight, my mother bought a lovely straw Easter bonnet for me. Usually careful in the extreme about the fit of my garments, somehow she slipped up on this particular hat. And the first time I wore it, she asked with tender concern: "Dear, is your new hat too tight for you?"

"No, Mother," I sighed philosophically, "it's all right *after* my ears go to sleep!"

That incident, the memory of my mother conducting the Easter cantata at church, Irving Berlin's song, "Easter Parade," and a passing interest in which of my friends made the Sunday rotogravure on a few Easters in particular, constitute the over-all meaning of the season to me until I was thirty-three years old. Aside from a rather characteristic eccentricity of refusing to buy a new hat until well *after* Easter, because the hoi-polloi bought bonnets at Easter, it was just another commercial holiday which I was asked to note in whatever radio show I happened to be writing in the spring of the year.

Now . . . *every morning is Easter morning to me!* I found

it easy to toss off the above lines of description of Easter B.C. in my life. Words become stubborn now as I struggle to combine them into some semblance of what I have discovered to be the true meaning of this glad time of the year.

First of all, when Easter morning breaks in all its light and glory upon my consciousness, it trails an unmistakable crimson cloud just lifted from the empty cross which my Lord left behind Him in order to "come back" to indwell me. I know His actual presence with me now *only* because He came out of that grave on the first Easter morning. If Jesus, the risen Christ, had not gone to be with the Father, the blessed Comforter — my Lord with me *now* — could not be here. Could not be there with you.

Just as Jesus must have swayed a moment on His wounded feet, as He stood in the mouth of the newly opened grave, adjusting His eyes to the sunlight of His own resurrection, so I sway in wonder at being able to share in this same resurrection today. Just as the nail prints were still in His hands and feet, so the scars of my own crucifixion with Him remind me that I *am* crucified with Christ. And am free because of it. The life I have discovered in Him has scars on it. But they are *glowing* scars because He lives *in me* now that the grave is open and empty.

Do we as Christians *live* every minute of our lives as though we really believe He came out of that tomb that first Easter morning? Do we live as though Easter is a legend or a reality? Do we let the world know that the very same power that brought Jesus Christ *out* of that heavy-shadowed blood and spice encrusted grave that first Easter morning *is operative in us today?* Do we live by the same power of God unto resurrection?

The Mary who loved Him so, Mary of Magdala, occupies a high place in my heart. I might have been that Mary. I love Him enough to have been that Mary. He forgave me for so much and I love Him according to that which I have been forgiven. My heart beats near hers now and I hope to be her close friend throughout eternity as we sit together at His beloved feet . . . pouring out our love before Him forever. I love Him for coming to her ahead of the others that first Easter morning. He did not love her *more,* but she was *there* looking for Him. And He honors those of us who are always seeking for new ways to tell Him of our love. He honors our seeking for more of Himself . . . for the sake of Himself. Mary of Magdala sought Jesus for Himself. She did not seek a blessing from Him. He was and *is* her blessing. As He is my blessing forever. I cannot ask for any other gift from Him. He dwarfs even His own gifts. My heart longs for more and still more of the Giver Himself. And this constant seeking for more of Jesus, for some new glimpse of Him, is one reason why every morning is an Easter morning for me.

And then, too, every morning is Easter morning to me because He lives within me every day. I could not believe in the actual physical resurrection of Jesus Christ *before* it took place in my own life.

I know He is risen now. He is with me minute by minute. My risen Master, my Lord . . . Rabboni! And I, too, go quickly and tell.

27.

I Am His
and
He Is Mine

I AM HIS AND HE IS MINE. That is my theology. It is very simple and I have discovered to my great and eternal joy that it works.

I did not become a Christian to save myself from eternal damnation. I did not become a Christian to make certain my passage to heaven. I did not think about either hell or heaven when I was being moved within by the Holy Spirit of Jesus Christ. Had I thought about them, I would not have been influenced by them because I did not believe they existed. I believe in them now, but *then* my attention was completely taken up mentally, emotionally and spiritually by the person of Jesus Christ. I was captivated by the One who holds "captivity captive."

I did not pick and choose among the various churches during the time the Holy Spirit bore down upon my brittle heart. I did not think much one way or another about churches. I had not been inside one in almost eighteen years and although I love them now and believe every new Christian *must* unite his life and efforts with some Christian group, at that moment when the Holy Spirit pressed in upon my sin-encrusted consciousness, I did not think of churches. I thought about Christ. And the more I thought about Him, the more real He became to me; and the more real He became, the more I wanted Him to be mine. And then my simple theology came into being. He seemed to say:

"I'll be yours if you'll be mine."

If you have read through this book, you know that my discoveries about the Christian life can be included in one sweeping over-all discovery:

I belong to Him and He belongs to me.

In the person of the Holy Spirit, my Lord is with me and in me as I work and play and laugh and weep and love on the earth. I am one of His sheep. I know His Name. I am His and He is mine.

It is His privilege and right to instruct me to do anything for His sake. I will go anywhere and do anything Jesus Christ asks me to do; and by His grace, I will do it calmly, willingly and quickly, because of who He is. He does not tell me to do something He cannot do.

I do not plead for Him to help me. I simply try to stay in position so He can work and love and serve *through* me. This is very restful for me *and* brings me into a climate of high excitement at one and the same time, since I am allowed to "rest" as His energy pours through me into the tasks He has set to be done.

There is no need for me to wonder whether or not He will get through to me in time to make ends meet. He is here "nearer than breathing and closer than hands and feet" every instant.

From the experience of this moment through which I am living as I write, "I am strengthened mightily by His Spirit in my inner self."

When the press of the crowds and the demands of people in trouble hack at my nerves, He whispers gently in my ear: "Leave them to Me, no one ever gets on My nerves."

When I am inclined to wonder if there will be enough material supply to go around, I am reminded that if He could create, He can maintain. Again . . . I need only to stay in position. I need only to keep my hands empty of myself and my own ideas, apart from Him.

I have discovered with great relief that the Father is like Jesus Christ. I must confess that for more than a year after I became a Christian, there was deep unrest in my heart as I tried to conceive a bloodthirsty Father who was so selfish that He would not take me, His creation, without forcing His only Son to suffer on the cross. I am not ashamed to admit that these thoughts haunted my dreams at night and blocked my flow of words from more than one platform as I spoke, until a short time ago. I believed in the death of Jesus Christ on the cross, but I resented God the Father for it because I loved Jesus so much.

Now, I see at last that the cross is on the very heart of God, the Father. It is clear to me now that God Himself *was* in Christ reconciling the world unto Himself. He tries in every possible way to approach us in ways we can understand. He came to earth and confined Himself within the feeble frame of man, in order to make Himself more approachable to us. The Israelites understood the blood sacrifice. God gave Himself in a way His people could understand. He must remain true to His own holiness. And when we, by faith, receive His Son, we receive the Spirit of the Sacrificial Lamb as well.

I am filled with joy and peace to have discovered that God, the Father, is not a bloodthirsty power. He is one with Jesus Christ. He showed us His own loving nature by sending His Son. He said in essence: "I am like my Son." Jesus said: "I and my Father are one."

I am also overjoyed to have discovered that my Lord is a jealous God. That He wants me all to Himself. But I am relieved to find that His jealous nature is unlike ours. He is jealous for our own good. He created us, and only He knows how we will function best and find the greatest joy. He demands that we follow His laws, *not* because He is an ogre and a stern, relentless Being. He wants us to obey Him because only He knows our hearts and only He knows what is for our good. I am glad He is jealous and I am also glad I have discovered why He is jealous.

I am also glad I have discovered directly from my own experience with Christ that Christianity is *not* something foreign and strange and unnatural, which must be forced upon me if I am to live it successfully. I have discovered that when I received Jesus Christ and when His work of redemption became a reality in my own life, I was transformed, *restored* to that relaxed, natural, childlike state when man first walked in the garden with the Father in the cool of the evening and talked with Him as a child talks lovingly with his parent. I am a "new creature," at home with her God.

Finally, and most blessedly, I have come upon the happy moment of discovery that this life hid with Christ in God is a *continuous unfolding*. It is not a creed to which I pledge myself and between whose rigid confines I must from thenceforth march. This new life in Christ is to me an eternal beginning. A fresh moment by moment unfolding as I walk moment by moment in the very presence of the One to whom I belong. I find that as long as I am aware of His presence, I am adequate for any event.

To my great, glad amazement, I have discovered that I am His and He is mine — forever.